The Ultimate "H

WRITING CO

Make Wade's "R.I.G." yours—Repetitive Income Generator

WADE COOK

How To Turn The Stock Market Into An Income Machine

ISBN 0-9745749-4-5
Library of Congress Cataloging-in-Publication Data
Cook, Wade
Stock Market Money Machine by Wade Cook

Published By
Liberty Network, Inc.
1420 NW Gilman Blvd., #2131
Issaquah, WA 98027
(425) 222-3760
(425) 222-3764 (fax)
www.wadecook.org
www.libertynetwork.us

Distributed to the trade by
Midpoint Trade Books
(212) 727-0190

Printed in the United States of America

To Brenda, Carrie, Leslie, Rachel and Benjamin.
I love all of you very much.

Dad

ACKNOWLEDGEMENT

Many thanks to my daughter, Brenda, my executive assistant and friend. Also to Craig McKenzie for helping me and our students get on track and keep on track.

I also have a grateful heart for my students who keep me going—prodding me along with suggestions and encouragement.

As always, my life is great because of my wife and mother of our children. My heart belongs to her.

TABLE OF CONTENTS

Financial Professionals Praise for Wade Cook i

Comments About Wade Cook. iii

Praise for Covered Call Strategy. v

Preface. ix

Chapter One—An Important Secret 1

Chapter Two—An Introduction to Writing Covered Calls 7

Chapter Three—Covered Call Classics 25

Chapter Four—Getting You Through the Covered Call
Learning Curve: Let's Do Some Deals 37

Chapter Five—What Makes Stocks Go Up and Down in Price . . . 51

Chapter Six—How Much Does It Take to Get Started?
Hint: $1,200 59

Chapter Seven—What is the Buy Back?. 71

Chapter Eight—Real Deals, Real Profits 77

Chapter Nine—The Effect of Earnings Season Reports 95

Chapter Ten—What Can You Do to Make More Money?
The Little Things That Make BIG Differences? 105

Chapter Eleven—Re-Allocate Your Assets. 111

Bonus Chapter—Ten Indisputable and Often
Gut-Wrenching Rules of Financial Success 115

Appendix 141

OTHER BOOKS BY WADE COOK

Real Estate Money Machine

Wade Cook's Stock Picking Handbook

Wall Street Money Machine

Mangosteen: Shocking Discoveries

Real Estate For Real People

101 Ways to Buy Real Estate Without Cash

How to Pick Up Foreclosures

Success American Style

Don't Set Goals

Wade Cook's Power Quotes

A+

Business Buy the Bible

UPCOMING RELEASES

Get in Touch With Your Inner Millionaire

Tax Strategies for Network Marketers

FINANCIAL PROFESSIONALS PRAISE FOR WADE COOK

"I am a financial planner who works primarily in mutual funds and life insurance. Any financial professional who criticizes Wade's strategies is simply speaking out of ignorance."

~ Christopher M., OH

"As a former financial planner, I thought I knew a lot about securities and the market. As a current attorney, I thought I knew a lot about companies and securities. Now I know I knew nothing about companies, securities and the market."

~ Michael R., WA

"I have 25 years experience as a broker with 3 major firms, and I was convinced I had nothing to learn from Wade Cook. How wrong I was! It was the most professional, dynamic and thoroughly enjoyable series of meetings I have ever attended. I plan to write my clients and advise them to seriously consider attending the next seminar. Once again, it was a profoundly educational seminar.

~ Carl G., CO

"Wade's books filled in the gaps in my stockbroker education. As a stockbroker I learned how the markets work but not how to personally make money. The firms I have worked for focus on selling and on customer service…not learning strategies beyond buy and hold. Thanks for showing me what I was missing."

~ Davis S., TX

"As a former stockbroker and current commodity broker, every thing I ever wanted to do to help people make money in the markets was here at Wade's seminar. This is a dream come true for me and I can truly explain how much of an impact was made on me today."

~ Richard M., FL

"I am a stockbroker. Most brokers know all about the workings of the stock market but little or nothing about helping clients make money. All Wade's strategies make sense and should allow me to better serve myself and my clients."

~ Bob B., CA

"I am a licensed broker (Series 6, 53 and Series 7) and, my position, I am a broker assistant for (a major bank). I have been employed there since June of '99. I took that job to learn about investing/money management, which I have since learned that they don't know. Thanks for teaching me in 3 days what they couldn't teach me in 8 months."

~ Derek S., MI

"I have a background as a stockbroker and have been investing for about 15 years. I thought I knew how to make money in the market, but I wasn't even close!"

~ Neil W., PA

COMMENTS ABOUT WADE COOK

"Wade Cook talks sense into dollars and cents. He is clear, understandable, and highly motivating. His first book *Real Estate Money Machine*, was original, creative, and very practical. I love it! *Real Estate for Real People* is even better. Read it! Do it!

~ Robert G. Allen
Author of *Nothing Down*

"One of Wades great abilities…is he's near genius way of taking something very complex and making it simple to understand and follow. This is what he has done in his lectures and books, and in his own financial deals. I am sure any reader would thoroughly enjoy, and most importantly benefit greatly financially from reading this book."

~ Mark Haroldson
Author of *The Courage to Be Rich*

"All my dreams can come true with Wade Cook strategies. He should be teaching at the Harvard Business School. They never taught me anything like this."

~ Jack C., CA

"A year ago we didn't know if we were going to keep this house. Today it's paid for. We've never lost a dime when we followed the rules…We had no background, Zero, Zip, Nada experience playing stocks before Wade. I don't think it's that he's done something new. What he's done is put it into plain language us common folk can understand."

~ Joel and Jennifer D., CA

"I feel like I have been reading by candlelight. Now, someone turned on the overhead light and I see the big picture.

~ Marie N., AL

"I turned $200,000 approximately into $1.2 million in 6 months."

~ Larry G., CA

“I trade full time (bought) 6 bedroom home with swimming pool and tennis court, helped others who need work (they work on my house now and I pay them with what I make in the market). I know if I lost everything, I could start with enough to buy one contract and make it from there.”

~ Garland H., FL

“I have spent a lot of money for my education of the stock market through the Wade Cook seminars and felt that in every class I got much more than my money’s worth. I have learned so much and have been able to take what I learned and make enough money to pay for the class… I feel I learned and experienced much more than I paid for.”

~ Rosalie W., WA

“This is the second time I have taken the class. I took the first one weeks ago and I have made $10,000! I have paid for the class! This works! I am living proof.”

~ Kim H., OR

PRAISE FOR THE COVERED CALL STRATEGY

"I purchased two stocks when I thought they were poised to take off. They did and when they started to downturn, I wrote covered calls on both stocks. About a week and half later, the third Friday came and went and I regained control of my stock. To my good fortune stocks began to rise again. I wrote a covered call on one and the other one spiked up so fast that when it started to downturn I sold the stock. In just under 30 days my brokerage account had gone from $5,000 to a whopping $11,600! Now I realize that this kind of return is somewhat of an anomaly, but the gains have not stopped. As of this writing it has been two and a half months since I bought my first stock and my brokerage account is at $15,000. I have tripled my money."

~ Robert Harris

"I am making approximately $7,000 a month with just your covered call strategy."

~Richard Lusco

"Starting in December and doing just six covered calls each month our base portfolio has increased 20% in value and our call premiums have been $4,500, $6,500 and $7,700 for rates of return 15, 22, and 26%. At this time we are able to help our youngest daughter and son-in-law on the down payment of their first house."

~ Donald and Joan Holicky

"I made $20,000 writing covered calls during the three weeks prior to the workshops using Wade's formula from the *Wall Street Money Machine*."

~ Gregory Martin

"I have made about $7,000 to $8,000 in one month writing covered calls. My wife was very skeptical, but she's a believer."

~ J. Brent Lewis

"In five minutes I calculated the premiums on covered calls on stock I own and on an annual basis it comes to $175,950. At today's listed options quotations, I have never done this or any other strategy besides buy and hold before. This is truly unbelievable!"

~James Ellis

"My favorite strategies are buying options on stock split companies and I really like covered calls. After 28 years with a well known company my wife took early retirement. We rolled her money over to a brokerage firm, and immediately did covered calls. Before retiring she was making around $1,000 per month on her 401 (K) plan. In October she made $7,756 doing covered calls and in November she make $7,180 in covered calls. I have an IRA account and I cleaned up in October of this year and I make about $2,500 per month. On the last 12 plays I did options and I haven't lost one yet. My goal is to make $100,000 the first year on my wife's account. I amazed myself in 5 months when she went over $25,000."

~ Lee Hamilton

"I am now a retired chiropractor at age 37…Averaging about $30,000 a month."

~ Alan P., AZ

"I currently make $8,000 to $15,000 per month. Thanks for changing my life."

~ Kathie L., CA

"I've made $7,000 to $10,000 per month since January."

~ Stephan H., CA

"Before Wade Cook info, I was trading with about 7-10% profit. Now I have increased that to 100-150% with a holding period of 5-7 working days."

~ Jonathan P., WA

"Our December statement showed that we had taken a $17,000 account to $120,000. In January we'd made (my husbands) annual salary plus a portion of mine."

~ Virginia M., NJ

"I found Wade in desperation. I invested approximately $100,000 in stock between a few lousy (I know this now) brokers. Within a whopping 6 months, I had a grand total of $50,000. Thanks to taking it upon myself to manage my money with Wade's strategies. I've earned $25,000 back I two months (while being very conservative)."

~ Michael B., CA

"I've made $100,000 + in five months starting with $5,000.

~ Ricky I., VA

"I actually have made almost the tuition cost before the class with the assistance of TST (Trading Skills and Techniques).

~ David D., NY

"Increased my account value from $25,000 to $160,000 in eight months."

~ Calis A., CA

"I have made $150,000 this year so far in Options, Covered Calls, and Puts."

~ Bijhan I., TX

"Using Stock Split Strategy #3 I bought three contracts of Qualcomm for $30,000. Overnight, the stock went up 167 points. Sold the February for $18,000."

~ Fred R., CA

"I had some experience with options because I had worked on the Commodity Exchange in New York (COMEX)—This workshop taught me so much more about using options & stocks. I think this is great, I just wish I had heard of this 10 years ago. I would be up front in the class teaching to everyone else. Thanks.

~ Dave R., NJ

"I am very encouraged by the Wade Cook Seminar System. Most people I talk to want to go out and make some things happen so they can afford the seminar and that is backwards because it will cost them money [not to go] and they may get discouraged and they won't get the education. I'm endorsing [the] Wade Cook seminars because every time I go to one, my income goes up. If my income is going up, why shouldn't I be excited? I'm writing covered calls, buying a few options and doing rolling stocks, just the basics. I am finding a 20-30% per month income. I am simply implementing the tools provided and the teachings by the staff at Liberty Network, Inc. Everyone thinks that there is an easy way out. I will tell you that I've never seen anything easier than following within the guidelines of the Wade Cook seminar system. Wade, in his wisdom and tenacity of going after knowledge and never letting down, has created something that will live a long time. We can provide for our family—generations and generations deep. This is SINCERE, REAL, DOABLE, can be done. Why waste another minute in your lives without seeing the potential and the fruit on the tree?

~ David E., FL

PREFACE

My wife asked me a very important question the other day. It really made me think. You see, normally I write the preface to a book after writing the bulk of the book. But her question changed that. This preface was written after about one half of the book was written.

It's important for you to know her question and my answer. The question was, "Why are you writing this book?" I looked quizzical. She continued, "I mean, what do you want the readers to get out of this book?" It really sounds like two questions, but she knows me very well. She knows of my passion to help others improve the quality of their lives. I want to help parents be better moms and dads. I want to help people give more time and money to their churches. I want to help people be more giving, more caring, more generous.

Many people think they have to wait to be wealthy to be generous. NO! Be generous and wait! I believe that our gracious God has wonderful things in store for us, if we would only ask him, "to be a lamp unto my feet and a light unto my path." (Psalms 119:5)

Money isn't everything, but if we keep our hearts and heads in the right place, it can sure help us accomplish a lot. So let me start by asking you a strange but wonderful question: "If you had a bit more money coming in, could you be a better you?" Here's another one: "What if money were not an issue, what would you do with your life?"

For almost three decades I've had the wonderful opportunity to meet tens of thousands of people. Their needs are real. Out of cash flow, tax write-offs and growth—the three reasons for investing—everyone needs more cash flow. The other reasons for investing can be dealt with in time. However, income generation is an elusive quest. Most people go to work and trade their time for income. Many are happy, many are not.

Since I'm asking questions here, let me continue: "What if, now watch this 'what if', you could have assets that would produce (give, generate, make, etc.) actual monthly income for you? Yes, even provide a paycheck. Most people have never thought of this. Most look forward to a lifetime of work—every day trading time, energy, skills for money. There has to be a better way, and there is. I've found it. It's a little known secret of the financial markets. It's easy to understand and accomplish. It's easy to get good at the process. There are simple steps, simple "how-to's". You do not yet know how much of a financial advantage you will have by knowing these steps.

This concept just keeps getting better, because you don't need a lot of extra cash to get started. Even $1,200 or so can get you going. Here's the point though: Each $5,000 you have will produce about $750 to $1,000 a month. Now, I'm pretty confident, after all my years of teaching, that you just read '$750 to $1,000 *a year*.' Everything becomes annual, in fact most financial institutions use "annual" because they haven't the foggiest idea that most of us need monthly income. Annual is nice, but monthly lets us pay the bills. So, to review, I wrote $750 to $1,000 per month—every thirty days. Pay the house payment, pay the bills, send the kids to college, travel and visit the grandkids. So, what are you thinking?

I hope you're thinking about moving on, moving up to a better life. If $5,000 produces $1,000, then $40,000 will produce between $6,000 and $8,000 a month. Want proof? This book is full of actual real world examples to get you there. And you know one of the greatest things about my secret simple strategy is that you can measure your rate of return (monthly or more)—the actual cash you'll receive—before you do the deal.

This formula can be worked at home, during coffee breaks, from your car or truck, or on vacation. You can start right where you are and use your work skills to base your decisions. If you're a nurse, home-maker, mill worker, truck driver, doctor or teacher, you take your knowledge and use it as a foundation.

I had a choice to make in teaching this wonderful cash flow strategy. One way to write is to use a "problem-solution" format. Most great novels use this methodology. This "problem-solution" or "conflict-resolution" is my choice. This brings up a new question or problem. Should I use artificial deals with made up companies and prices, OR should I use real deals from the real world?

What would you have me do? Students all over the country would rather use real deals. They want to see money made in the market with Intel, Oracle, Microsoft and EBAY. It's all a lot more interesting this way.

For you, the reader, please realize that every price used here was real. It was a snapshot in time. Everything is a process, including the strategy used, how we found a stock, how we chose what to sell. The prices used are probably long gone by the time you read this book. However, the processes are the same.

I'll use various amounts of money—sometimes $10,000, sometimes $20,000, but usually $40,000 for our examples. Here's why. The average American family can live on $44,000—about $4,000 per month. And that worker has FICA and other amounts held out. The income made in this book is unearned income. Income taxes are due, but the other withholdings are minimized.

$40,000 will buy $80,000 worth of stock, if purchased on margin. $80,000 will generate $8,000, sometimes even $9,000 to $12,000 per month. That's DOUBLE what the average family needs to live on. Again, I'll prove this throughout this book. I'll show it daily on T.S.T.(Trading Skills and Techniques), at our internet site at www.wadecook.org. Again, the trades are real to show you that you can do it.

If you want to make millions, this is the wrong book. However, if you want to make enough money to live nicely on, then I think you'll like this easy-to-use method. When I wrote my first book, the publisher said, "Wade, we've got dozens of books on how to make millions. Can you write a book on how to make a living?" Yes, and I'll go one better. I'll write here on how to make a great living—in 1 to 2 hours a week. The rest of the time is used to explore, discover, visit, build, grow—to BE.

I surely don't need to tell you what you need money for—you know. Everyone has needs. For example, one retired couple just needs an extra $800 a month. A mother with a dyslexic child needs $2,200 a month for a special school. A man near 50 wants to give $1,200 a month to his retired parents. A couple in Jacksonville wants to support a Christian orphanage in Jamaica and needs $8,000 a month. A doctor wants to go to Moscow and work in their medical clinics. He needs $20,000 for medicine and hired help. Big John, age 34, needs $12,000 for an operation for his father.

All of these needs are real, personal and important. I can't help everyone, but the few who read my books and attend my seminars know of my passion to help people live lives of compassion. I hope I can help you.

So, why do I write? I'm not writing to become someone. I'm writing because in thirty years in the financial industry, and of all the methods of investing I know, what you'll read here is the <u>best</u>, the <u>easiest</u>, and the <u>most sure way</u> for you to get your money working for you and not you working for your money.

You want results, I'm here to help.

CHAPTER ONE
AN IMPORTANT SECRET

You are now reading about a little known, seldom used street-tested method for building up filthy-rich type income. More money than you can spend. It doesn't take a lot to get started and it's relatively easy to learn and master.

It's a secret, or so it would seem. It's powerful in its simplicity.

Imagine if you will, a world—your world—where you do not have to work. You live on and are supported by an income source that very few know about. In this world you spend your time with family and friends, helping at church, developing talents. You drive a nice car, all paid off. You have no mortgage—or at least this income source lets you double and triple your payments, and you're debt free in a few years. Yes you pay off your credit cards every month. You're free financially. Money is not a problem. You're liberated and may now move on and develop skills and attributes most only dream of.

Imagine this world in six months to a year. And know that you need very little money, and very little time to get these huge checks coming in. The secret, the system is Writing Covered Calls.

LET ME INTRODUCE MYSELF. . .

My name is Wade Cook. I am a cash flow educator. I write books and put on seminars. I love to teach and help people. I get nothing out of what they do. My passion is to help people be better parents, give more to their churches and live quality lives—lives close to God—lives with purpose. Money is just a tool.

I made my first million in real estate. My activities and my books, *Real Estate Money Machine, How to Pick Up Foreclosures,* and *101 Ways to Buy Real Estate Without Cash,* set the real estate investing world upside-down. Today, many other books and seminars are based on my methods. Now, I've moved on to Treating the Stock Market Like A Business. My books on stock market investing, *Wall Street Money Machine,* and *Stock Market Miracles* were both on the New York Times Business Best Seller List. I don't break the rules, I re-write them.

Why is this important to you? I'm in the trenches doing deals—making money. I try and test strategies. I develop and design monthly income systems for the busy mother and business executive. I have discovered a new system for becoming cash flow wealthy. I've spent twelve years dissecting, poking, prodding and with real money I've worked out the bugs. This secret new system is truly effective and efficient. It will soon become your Repetitive Income Generator. And I'm confident this RIG will move you along the highway to great wealth—wealth with monthly checks coming in for you and your family.

THREE REASONS FOR INVESTING

The foundational concept for all investment and business activities is to make money. There are three ways: (1) Build up income; (2) Create Tax Write-offs; and (3) Growth or Equity build-up. Of these three, CASH FLOW is the paramount reason. With excess cash flow you can buy tax-sheltered investments and you will have the luxury to wait for growth.

But it's cash flow that let's you quit your job, go back to school, be with your kids and grandkids, travel, explore, discover. Cash flow is the financial freedom engine.

MY THIRD WAY

For millennia people have built wealth one of two ways: (1) Buy assets, say $1,000,000 worth, and pay it off; or (2) start a business (any idea—product or service) and nurture it to be worth millions. Some make it, many fail.

Let's go back to our world of income. I've found a better, easier, more certain way—what I call A THIRD WAY. The first two take too long, are fraught with peril and present too many heartaches and headaches.

Let's look at $1,000,000. This much money in the bank would make $30,000 a year. Not much for an average family. What if I could show you how to make this much with $8,000 to $15,000 (in stock assets) and even show you how to start with $500 to $1,200 and build to this amount? Are you getting this? You are possibly very close to retiring.

Also, imagine a guide who is in the minefield with you leading the way. No pointing out the path. No maps for sale, BUT, take my hand and let's get across together.

Writing covered calls requires three things: (1) stock—in one hundred share batches, (2) options—that we sell to generate income, and (3) a bit of knowledge to put it together.

HOW IT WORKS

We own or buy stock on companies that we like. We then sell a call option against our stock, giving someone the right to buy our stock at a price we like. Is this cool or what? We get paid cash from all those risky option investors, just for giving them the right to buy our stock, whether they buy it or not.

Example: We buy 1000 shares of a stock for $4.80 per share, or $4,800. Note: with margin we only have to put up 50% of this, or $2,400. Our broker puts up the rest and uses the stock as collateral. It's February, and we sell the March $5 call options for 60¢. Options expire on the third Friday of each month. By doing that, we take $600 into our account—in one day. It's our money. We can spend it, buy more stock—whatever we want. It's that simple. $2,400 has given us an asset where we make $600 for one month.

One of three things will now happen. The stock will go up, stay the same, or go down. If the stock stays the <u>same</u>, we won't sell it. We keep the $600 and still own the stock. We now sell the April options for another $700. The stock moved up a bit.

If the stock goes <u>down</u> (you need to learn protective strategies) we keep the $600 and sell the April options or wait for the stock to rise and sell them later. Whichever we do, we make more money.

If the stock goes up, we sell the stock for $5.00. Hmm…$4.80 to $5.00 is 20¢ times 1000 shares, and we make another $200, totaling $800. That's $800 on our $2,400 investment.

THINK! If you had four positions like this, $10,000 would bring in $3,000 this month—that's $36,000 a year. We've already beat the interest payment on one million dollars in the bank!

Now obviously with any strategy there are ways to enhance it, tweak it, and even make more. Here's a tracking system on Star Scientific (STSI). I have $5,285 tied up and it's making me about $2,000 a month. In 3 months my $5,285 has grown to $12,035. I have many positions like this. I do these all the time and invite you to look diligently at this chart.

STSI Cash Flow Tracking Sheet.

$6,750 Cash Flow

$5,285 Invested

$12,035 Current*

Stock (co)		Star Scientific		Ticker	STSI	Total Ca[sh] Taken In		
Date		# shares		Cost		On margin		
1/31	B	1000	$4.54	$4,540		Batch 1		
2/3	B	1000	$6.03	$6,0[3]		[B]atch 2		
			Totals	$10,5				
Date	B or S	#Contracts	Month	Strike		Cash in/out	Net	

From 1/3/05 to 4/12/05 Wade has done 6 round trip trades on STSI producing $1,850

Date	B or S	#Contracts	Month	Strike	Premium	Cash in/out	Net	Total
4/12	S	20	May	5c	$1.00	$2,000		
4/20	B	20	May	5c	($0.50)	($1,000)	$1,000	$2,850
4/26	S	20	June	5c	$0.90	$1,800		
4/27	B	20	June	5c	($0.50)	($1,000)	$800	$3,650
4/27	S	20	June	5c	$0.90	$1,800		
5/16	B	20	June	5c	($0.45)	($900)	$900	$4,550
5/23	S	20	June	5c	$0.70	$1,400		
6/7	B	20	June	5c	($0.60)	($1,200)	$200	$4,750
6/7	S	20	July	5c	$1.00	$2,000		
						$0	$2,000	$6,750

*This figure represents the amount of cash flow generated from writing covered calls added to the current value of the stock on margin as of the close of the market on 6/14/2005 of $4.92 if no money is taken out of the account. The S & B means sell and buy. This is what we call double-dipping.

WORTHY OF THE EFFORT

I don't want to waste time—mine or yours. If $10,000 will make $3,000 to $4,000 a month, do you see your retirement? $1,000 will make $300 to $400 a month. Can you use the extra money? Build it up to $100,000 (or sell one of your rental houses) and it will make $20,000 to $30,000 a month. Look at this brief list—proof of profits:

Stock	Cash Invested	Cash in to Date	Time	Round Trip
STSI	$5,285	$6,750	18 weeks	10.5
STSI	$7,810	$6,510	18 weeks	55
IDCC	$4,618	$1,150	1 Week	1.5
NFLX	$32,483	$27,720	42 weeks	20
RMBS	$10,062	$4,690	26 weeks	9.5
TASR	$9,142	$5,815	26 weeks	14.5

"I started with $380 using Wade's strategies,...buying calls on slams, buying calls on stock splits, buying stocks and writing covered calls. I have increased my portfolio to over $25,000.

—Jeff N., MO

Please read this again. Do you have anyone in your life that can help you take $380 and build it to $25,000? Well, do you? This is an important question. I didn't promise Jeff that he could do this, and I won't promise you either, but I will give you a fighting chance to take control of your financial destiny. I can show and teach you how to work the process. It's up to you, choose your associations wisely.

This is my THIRD WAY. It's a Repetitive Income Generator or RIG as I like to call it. It takes about three to five hours a month—more if you want to make more. I love this strategy. It's a STOCK MARKET MONEY MACHINE.

So, why is it that some people feel unequal to this new way of life?

- Some say they can't learn…well, put your mind at rest. You can learn this. Old dogs learn new tricks all the time.

- Some say, "They've seen it all before." I'm sorry, they haven't seen this. Options are too risky. Typical investing doesn't produce this level of income. This is an easy-to-learn, easy-to-implement system with "do's and dont's", rules and formulas and education to enhance and safeguard profits.

- Some say they can't spend all day watching a computer screen and charting. Okay, throw away the computer—just kidding. Use it to link to us. We'll help in more ways than you know. You live your life. Seriously, this takes one to five hours a month.

- Some just don't believe they can live rich, live large. In this book you'll learn how to get the fish jumping in your boat. Some people put self-constructed obstacles in the way. They've resigned themselves to living small. Skepticism is healthy to a certain extent, but many cling so hard to doubt and fear, that their arms tire, and they fail to grasp a new opportunity. My THIRD WAY is not just a simple idea, but a time-honored WAY to build a new wonderful life. Don't judge this simple system by where you are, but by where this book (and my educational processes) can get you. This is a wonderful cash flow system.

Yes, you can do it. You can do it starting where you are. You can do it in this market. There's income waiting. It's yours for the taking.

CHAPTER TWO
AN INTRODUCTION TO WRITING COVERED CALLS

Over the years I've asked some very important questions--usually in marketing pieces. These questions were meant to get people's attention. They were designed to promote thought, to get people really thinking about their financial situation.

I firmly believe that the quality of our lives is based on two things: (1) the quality of the people we associate with, and (2) the quality of the questions we ask. At a seminar someone asks: "Is this XYZ stock a good stock to buy?" It's an okay question but not a quality question.

Let me go back a little farther--to my real estate days. When *Real Estate Money Machine* was my bestselling book, I went on a PR tour. At a seminar, a woman would ask, "Is buying this duplex a good idea?" I would ask back, "I'm not sure, what else could you be doing with your time and money?" She would answer, "Oh, I don't know. The duplex needs about $15,000 of repairs and then even if fully rented it will lose about $600 a month." She came to this conclusion herself.

People need to really think about such important decisions. Surely, the quality of the answer with all its ramifications depends on the quality of the question. Do you want to notch up your life? Then notch up the quality of your questions.

QUESTION #1: CAN THE STOCK MARKET BE THE ANSWER TO YOUR CASH FLOW NEEDS?

Before we get to the answer specifically, let's expand the thought process behind this question. What if you could find a way to make the stock market your employer? Once or twice a month **it** would send you a check for $5,000! What if all this took you three to six hours a month? And what if risk and exposure were minimized?

When I pose scenarios like this, you have to know that I have something up my sleeve. I know a secret that very few know. In fact, most retail stockbrokers may have heard of my secret, but the extent of their knowledge is 'Pick a card, any card.' They do not have a passion for helping their clients develop actual, spend-able monthly income. Without this passion, they'll never gain the precision to make it happen. Without the passion and precision no one will capture the profits--our third "P" in this triumvirate of success. However, cash flowing assets—real, spend-able cash—is all I think about in the financial side of my life. You benefit because this secret can be learned, easily implemented in a short amount of time, and duplicated repeatedly.

Now, back to the question about the Stock Market being a solution to generate more income than you can spend.

The answer to the question would have to be an emphatic "NO" if you only knew about and used old, worn out and stale buying strategies. There simply is not much in a typical investor's brain except buy and hold. Now, I have no bad words for buy and hold. To me, it's a great way to generate wealth down the road. I just don't see it as a way to generate income in the good old "here and now".

Everyone has their opinion about the stock market; however, rarely does anyone see it as a way of getting a second, third or fourth monthly check. So here's the solution, my secret, if you will: **Use your stock as a**

foundation upon which to build income. Sorry to be redundant, but this is real cash income—take it out to pay your bills each month. It's called "**writing covered calls**". It's about selling for cash, wild, risky stock options to all those crazy people who like to buy them. Let's get back to the "second paycheck" by moving on to the next quality question.

QUESTION #2: DO YOU KNOW HOW TO GET A SECOND PAYCHECK WITHOUT GETTING A SECOND JOB?

I remember a story a few years ago about a young college football running back. The coach felt the player had the skills, but on every attempt he'd get hammered. Finally the coach called him over and said, "Boy, run where they ain't!"

Writing covered calls is a very powerful strategy, but it flies in the face of conventional wisdom. You must be prepared to walk alone even in the face of critical questioning.

To illustrate, let's look at a basic example. Not every stock has options, so from now on only purchase stocks that have options (all of the big ones do) and buy stock in one hundred share batches.

You own 800 shares of XYZ. You purchased these shares for $12 each. The cost of $9,600 was spent in the hope that the shares would increase in value. The company hasn't paid out any dividends so far, but they might do so in the future. Rumors abound that they're thinking of paying dividends and that's one reason the stock went from $13 to $14. You're up $2. You're feeling pretty good, but you now need some money for your daughter's college books, tuition, etc. It all adds up. You consider selling some stock, maybe one hundred shares or so. You really think the stock will go up more—in fact, this morning it went up 20 cents to $14.20—so you're reluctant to sell. Problem? You still need a little extra cash.

You then can call your broker and ask what the $15 Calls are going for in February, for example. In this senario, it's currently December 5th. The call options are going for $1 x $1.10. That's the bid ($1) and ask ($1.10). Basically, you sell at the BID and buy at the ASK. You're not happy with $1, so you put the order in to sell the option for $1.20. The stock would have to move up another 40 cents or so for you to get filled at $1.20. A few days pass. The stock backed off of $14.20, about 10 cents, but two days later it moved up nicely and you are confirmed on the sale of the option at $1.20. That generates for you $960 (800 shares x $1.20) which is in your account the next day. You then ask your broker to send a check for $900. The slowest part of this whole transaction is the US Postal Service.

Now, what have you done? Stock options (for all those weird buyers out there) give the owner the right, but not the obligation, to buy a stock at a set price on or before the expiration date. But, you didn't buy an option—you sold an option. You have written a covered call. To write means to sell. Selling generates cash and for the receipt of this cash you have agreed to sell your stock at $15. "Your stock" is the next item of discussion. You own the stock, so if someone (you don't know who this mysterious someone is) buys your stock, you own enough of it to sell.

A "call" is one of two types of options. A "put" is the other type. Typically, you buy a call when you think a stock is going up; you buy a put when you think a stock is going down.

However, we're not playing options, hoping for something to happen. We're not putting market forces to work against us. We're not gambling. What we are doing is going for certain cash flow. We needed money and in one day we generated $960.

Now, what will happen? One of three things:

1. The stock will go above $15 and we will have it taken away from us in the form of a sale. I call this "getting called out". Three trading days later, $12,000 (800 x $15) hits your account. Not bad. $9,600 to $12,000, plus the extra $960.

2. The stock stays below $15, even as close as $14.95, and the options expire. You still own the stock and you still get to keep the $960. You got paid to take on the obligation to deliver the stock, but you didn't need to sell it.

3. Whether the stock goes up (above $15), stays the same or goes down, you can always buy back the option and end the trade. This "buy back" opens up a wonderful world of cash flow possibilities. It only takes 13 to 18 seconds to do, but the ramifications and possibilities are incredible.

Many parts of this book are about generating more income with this position. In fact, let's have a party! Think, you have just generated $960 that you didn't know was possible. Your broker will be impressed. Let's call this party a BBQ—**B**igger, **B**etter, **Q**uicker. More Income, Faster Income, Multiple Rivers of Income™.

For now, just realize my secret is out. Whatever you paid for this book, a fraction of one trade makes it worthwhile. Before we move on, let me ask you a personal question: If you can generate $960 a month (2 weeks to 7 weeks), then how may XYZ stocks do you need? Four? Eight? Is it time for a major garage sale? Many of you are three to six months from retiring—and I mean retiring cash flow wealthy!

QUESTION #3:
CAN YOU GET YOUR MONEY WORKING AS HARD AS YOU WORK?

You can make this a job if you want to, but you're already busy. You don't need another job. You do, however, need more income. This second paycheck is nice and it is certain.

To answer our question #3, let's do another deal. This will illustrate how to trade on an investment.

While looking around at various stocks, you notice that similar priced stocks have vastly dissimilar option prices. Remember the old adage: "The greater the risk, the greater the reward; the lower the risk, the lower the reward."

My day goes something like this: It's about one hour after the market has opened. That's about 7:30am Pacific Time. I've finished playing basketball. I got whacked pretty hard upside the head during the game. I hope the market is gentler! I now take time to look at some stocks. I do most of my trading on a cell phone. I don't think you absolutely have to use a computer, if you don't want to.

The trades we look at will be from scratch, meaning we'll shop around, check prices, look at a few charts, check option prices, and then move on if we feel right about it.

Here are a few choices:

Company	Ticker	Stock Price	Strike Price	Bid & Ask
Star Scientific	STSI	$5.62	July $5	1.10 x 1.30
Sisteon Corp.	VC	$7.60	July $7.50	.75 x .85
Decode Genetics	DCGN	$7.63	July $7.50	.85 x .95
Able Labs.	ABRX	$4.47	July $5	.60 x .70
Netflix Inc.	NFLX	$14.59	July $15	.70 x .80
Micron Tech.	MU	$10.94	July $10	1.15 x 1.20
			July $11	.45 x .50
Ameritrade Hldg.	AMTD	$15.13	July $15	1.05 x 1.15
			July $17.50	.20 x .30
Advance Micro Dev.	AMD	$16.66	July $16	1.25 x 1.30
			July $17	.65 x .70
Myriad Genetics	MYGN	$16.41	July $15	1.80 x 1.90
			July $17.50	.50 x .60

Okay, I've been doing this for years, so my eyes are automatically drawn to Advanced Micro Devices and Star Scientific. Before proceeding, I'd like to mention three things:

(1) **These prices are a snapshot in time. These prices and their accompanying option prices change constantly.** I pose these here for your learning benefit. I teach formulas, and then find a stock or option to fit the formula. One of the cardinal rules in writing books or doing seminars on topics of finance is to not use mathematics—numbers bog people down, but we must use numbers. Numbers tell the story—and cash numbers are what

you can use for a car payment. Stick with the numbers. I'll try to make them understandable.

(2) **I never make recommendations. The actual trade is between you and your stock broker.** I may say I like a stock. I have a right to do that, and I will tell of trades I've done, past tense, but again, for educational purposes only. You take the risk; you make the profits or experience the losses. I sell books and teach seminars. I get nothing out of what you do.

(3) **$10,000 equals $2,000 per month.** This is a very important point. In all I do, in all of my seminars, I try to tell and show people how to get a 20% cash-on-cash return monthly income. I don't always do it, but I attempt to reach that goal. To do so requires a high level of involvement and a tad bit more risk. So, for some of you, how's this for a target? "$10,000 equals $1,000 per month." If you could do this consistently, how would that change your life? Are the results worth the effort?

So . . . Let's make some money. Soon you'll be amazed at the ease of doing this. You'll be asking yourself why your broker hasn't told you about covered calls. You'll realize how much cash has been left on the table these past months and years.

GO FOR THE CASH

Let's start with Navarre Corporation (NAVR). The stock was $7.98. Today is a 1 ½ weeks to June option expiration. We'll look at selling the July calls. The $7.50 calls for July are $1.05 by $1.10. Again we'll sell at the bid (a market order) which I don't always do. I might put it out (an order to sell or OTS) at a higher price. For this example, we'll take what the market will give us.

Also, in our example, we'll do the stock purchase on margin, meaning we'll only have to put up half of the cash. The brokerage firm will loan the balance at a relatively small interest rate.

We will purchase 1000 shares of NAVR at $7.98, for a total of $7,980. One-half for margin would be $3,990. That is our cash into the deal, our asset. Now, what about the cash flow?

We can sell 10 contracts (one contract equals 100 shares) at $1.05 each, or $1050. That is calculated by multiplying 1000 shares by $1.05. However you calculate it, you are taking in $1050 and agreeing to sell the stock at $7.50 per share.

I'm sure you're asking, "Why are we buying the stock at $7.98 and agreeing to sell it at $7.50? Aren't we going to lose money, $480 to be exact?" ($7980 - $7500). The answer is yes. Why would we do that? Let's explore.

This strategy is called selling an in-the-money call. Strike prices for options are fixed. Stock prices move all the time. Why sell in the money? Simply put, to pick up the $1050. We have $1050 hitting our account. The brokerage firm's computer will just recognize this as cash. It can be taken out; it can be used for other investments; it can be applied to our margin requirement.

Here I'd like to mention Stop Loss Orders. We will put a stop loss order in place on the stock at $7.20 or $6.90. I'll go into detail on this in another section.

Now, let's move on to the expiration date in July. If the stock stays above $7.50, we'll get called out. That's my jargon for "we'll sell the stock". We don't have to do anything to have this happen. It will all happen electronically and automatically. We will have a stock sale and three trading days later the money for selling the stock will be in our account.

Here's another phrase I've developed: "You'll have to 'give back' $480." I realize on your tax return it will be a capital loss of $480 ($7980 minus $7500) and option income of $1050, but just for educational purposes in this book, we'll just say we're giving back $480 of the $1050. Our profit (before commission) is $570. Does a $570 cash return on a $3990 investment feel good to you? How about $500 cash on $3,950? Does $10,000 making actual cash money of $1,000 start to seem possible? (Half of the $7,980)

If you decide you don't want to sell the stock (get called out) there are other alternatives that will be discussed later on.

ELAN Corporation (ELN) is a pharmaceutical company. I have high hopes for this company. Who knows? Let's see if this stock will work.

Purchase 1,000 shares at $6.76, or $6,760. One half of that amount on margin would be $3,380. So we only spend cash out of our pocket. The stock is slightly below the $7.50 strike price. In this price range, strike prices go in $2.50 increments, i.e. $2.50, $5, $7.50, $10, $12.50, $15, $17.50, $20, $22.50 and $25. Most stocks, once they've hit a $25 strike price, go in $5 increments, i.e. $25, $30, $35, $40, and so on. There are a few exceptions to this rule.

The July $7.50 calls on ELN are .45 cents by .50 cents. We can wait to get more, but while waiting, time elapses. We're selling time and volatility. To continue, .45 cents times 1000 shares equals $450 on our $3,380 purchase. The "powers-that-be" hate it when I use rates of returns, so you figure it out yourself. Just divide $450 by $3,380 or $450 by $6,760 if you don't use margin. One Month? Not bad and we're not finished. The stock will go up, or down or stay the same. Let's explore each scenario.

UP: The stock can go up a little and nothing will happen. If it goes over $7.50, and stays there, we will get called out. We can always "buy-back" this call before we're called out and have the stock to fight another day.

For July, though, what if it's above $7.50? Our stock gets sold (called out) and we make another $740 ($7,500 - $6760) on our stock. Now our profits are $1,190 ($740 + $450), minus commissions. Now figure your rate of return. Keep practicing and get ready to retire!

DOWN: If the stock goes down, we don't get called out. We can buy back the $7.50 calls before expiration and sell out another month, and wait for the next upturn. Or, the $7.50 call option could just expire on the expiration date. Now look out to the next month. Also consider the story-line of the stock. Is it still worth owning? Has there been news that would encourage you to move to another stock?

SAME: Same as Down. Time elapses. The option price gets cheaper. We can do nothing; buy back the option; sell the stock; wait it out and sell options out the next month (February) or even further out in the year.

You're getting in control of your financial destiny.

NETFLIX (NFLX). As of this writing, Netflix is going for $14 per share. So, up front, do you see that if we sell the $15 calls on 1,000 shares we'll gain $1 or $1,000? However we're going to take in $1,200 ($1.20 times 1000). $1000 subtracted from $1200 leaves $200. $200 on $14,000, or if on margin, $7,000, is an okay return.

UP, DOWN, or the SAME—Good thing, with writing covered calls, we can calculate our cash return before we ever enter the trade. Just make that phone call to get prices, start exploring and **practice trade**. (For more information on Practice Trading call us at 866-579-5900.

And you do not yet know about buy-backs, double-dipping, roll-outs and several more power strategies—to make even more money..

Let me share a story of a previous student named Karl. He started with $18,000 in the market. Over a 3-4 month period he grew the account to about $80,000. He played straight options and got involved during a very bullish period in the market.

He approached his wife and wondered if he could quit his job. "Look", he said, "at all the money I've made!" He was 58 years old. Like any spouse, husband or wife, there is always the fear of the unknown. Most of us have grown so attached to our security blankets. Some of you can probably relate to this couple's predicament.

I'm amazed at how many 50 and 60 year olds will work at a job they detest or have outgrown because of their employer sponsored medical insurance. They'll work 5 to 15 more years because of $680 per month. I wonder if one covered call a month—certain income—could alleviate these concerns? Fear is real. Developed skills and actual results are the antidote.

Let's get back to Karl's story. His wife simply said, "Do it again." A wise challenge and guess what? He couldn't, or at least he didn't. In fact he treaded water. Then he moved upward and onward. He was one of my workshop attendees, where we spend the largest portion of time on "Writing Covered Calls."

Karl took about $50,000, bought good stocks, and started writing covered calls. One month he'd net $7,000, the next $9,000. He "double-dipped" a few times and all in all netted about $8,000 per month for eight months. He went to his wife with his records and showed her how he had been making this kind of money.

Now she was willing, even eager, to have him retire. The difference was that he was moving in a new direction—with skills, confidence and real results. Did you catch the numbers? $8,000 on average for 8 months is $64,000. That's less than his big pop of $80,000. So what's the difference? Steady, consistent, workable, achievable monthly income.

Truly, Karl's knowledge and developed skills moved him to a whole new phase of his life. He was trading on his good investments. He's making his investments work for him, not the other way around. This leads me to my next question:

QUESTION #4:
DO YOU KNOW HOW TO GET ASSETS TO PRODUCE INCOME?

For years I've stood in front of audiences and presented a series of questions. My intent was to get them to question a financial myth: That being wealthy equals cash flow. The truth is, many people have to work hard, even take on extra work, to support their assets.

I demonstrate in my seminars, and hold out both hands like bowls. I tell the audience I hold assets in my left hand, and my right hand holds income. I then ask them which is more important, assets or income? Most say income, but a few murmur assets. So before it goes too far, I ask, "What lets you retire, go back to school, travel, pay off your home, etc.? Now the response is unanimous—Income.

Next, I ask the audience, "Can you have income without assets?" NO. Some one or some thing has to produce the income. We cannot have income without assets. I follow with another question, "But can you have assets without income?" Heads start to nod all over the room. "In fact," I continue, "many of you have far too many assets that mean nothing in the way of income."

Trying to be a bit humorous, I continue, "I'm sure all of you have heard of income producing assets. For most of you, you're it. You are your only income producing asset—and if your asset doesn't go to work, when will your income stop?" The audience responds with a few chuckles.

However, this is a major point. This is also the major problem with most wealth enhancement programs. It's about people, in most cases you, the individual, going to work—trading time for money. Even if you own your own business, you're still trading time for money. All of us need to get our money producing money. We need to get this financial car on the road, keep it moving, fix a flat tire or two, take a few detours, but keep it moving, keep it producing income. Oh, and we will get better at this. It's not that the job becomes easier; it's that our ability to do the job gets better.

I want to share with you what I want out of a business, but if we can't take home real money, it serves no immediate purpose, so let's do a deal and keep the cash rolling in.

Buy on dips, sell on strength. More completely this reads, buy the stock on dips (temporary, short term down ticks), sell the call on strength.

TIVO (TIVO) was at $4.90. I bought 1000 shares. This cost $4,900, but only $2,450 on margin. Another point about margin: As you gain experience and have a little more cash in the account, your margin can go to 30%—meaning in this case you'd only have to have 30% of $4,900 (or about $1,650) in your account.

TIVO was wandering between $4.80 and about $5.10. The $5 call for one month out was 30 cents, or a total of $300 for 10 contracts. I waited about 5 days for the stock to move up to $5.10, and then sold the $5 call for 55 cents or $550. As of this writing the stock was at $5.60. If it stays above $5, I will get called out. I will make $650, minus commissions (about $90 for three commissions).

Before we move on, let me do a brief buy back and roll out. I want to ease you into this type of double play. On Thursday before the Friday expiration date, the stock is $5.60 per share. I've changed my mind; I don't really want to sell the stock right now. To "buy-back" means to undo the covered call. To effectuate this, I BUY 10 contracts of the $5 call option for that same month. The $5 call option is going for .65 x .70. It will cost me $700 (.70 x 1,000 shares) to end my obligation to sell the stock. I'm underwater $150, ($700 minus the original $550 I took in for selling the call originally).

Now, I have a few choices. One choice is to do nothing. Wait for the stock to rise more, sell it or sell another call option at the same strike price or even the next strike price up—the $7.50's. I could also just go ahead and sell the next month out calls right now. Before I show you this, let me state one of my almost always true truisms: "*Whatever it costs to buy back the option now, you can always sell it for more further out.*"

Remember, we're selling time. You're buying back an option with two days of time left and selling an option with 31 days of time left. Point: when we buy options the deterioration of the time value in the option hurts us, but when we sell options, time works for us—we pre-capture now all the time in the premium. We're starting to act like a high-paid option trader. We're harnessing market forces and using these forces to our benefit.

Back to TIVO. Actually we had it pre-set and when the program is on, we'll pick it up. Sorry, a little TIVO humor there. Okay, 70 cent premium costs us $700, BUT, now get this, THE FEBRUARY OR NEXT MONTH OUT $5.00 CALL IS GOING FOR $1.10. The $7.50 call is also 30 cents. That would be interesting: sell the next month out $7.50 calls for $300. We're back in the positive. The stock can go up. I think it would be great to have to worry about getting called out at $7.50. $4,900 to $7,500 would be a nice profit.

But, back to reality, this stock has struggled with the $6.00 price. The $1.10 premium means $1,100. That sounds good. We go from being down $150 to being up $950 ($1100 - $150). $950 is a nice two month return on our $2,450.

However, we want a little more. If the stock moves up to $5.80 or $5.90 quickly, we could possibly get $1.30 premium. The order is placed to sell the $5.00 calls at $1.30 GTC (Good Till Cancelled). It could be a day order, but let's have a little patience. Sure enough, three days later we get filled at $1.30. Our account takes in $1,300. Even though the $7.50 calls hit 40 cents, we wanted the larger premium on the $5 strike price. For us, it's about steady and more certain cash flow.

Just one more trade. We take in the $1,300 and two days later this stock sells off 80 cents from $6.00 to $5.20. The $5 call drops to 40 cents. We then can buy it back for $400 and end the obligation. A week later, it's back up to $5.85 and we again sell the $5 calls for 90 cents or a total of $900.

I know I got carried away. I love double-dipping. There is an entire section on buy backs coming up. This is what I do. I've done this five times in one month on two different stocks (NFLX and QCOM). That's a lot of profits, and I felt great! This feeling is my financial high. I hope to show you how to do this.

Is this starting to turn into a business for you? Consider the following:

BUSINESS

WHAT I WANT

A) I want the **freedom** of owning my own business and not having to punch a time clock.
B) I want **a lot of income** with small expense, not the other way around.
C) I want unlimited potential – with my only limitation being my creativity, my industry, myself.
D) I want tax reductions and write-offs, growth of assets and **excessive income** from the assets.
E) I want to set aside huge amounts of tax deductible money for my future. I also want to make money in a tax-deferred account.
F) I want more quality time to be together with my family and friends.
G) I want a small business with **big profits**. "Stay small and keep it all."
H) I want **easy access**, low start up costs and a way to grow the business without huge advertising costs.
I) I want to share with family and friends, and mentally, not financially support each other.
J) I want the ability to wind down, sell, quit or just walk away at my choosing.
K) I want to be **happy** with the process—and to use my knowledge of things to connect the dots.
L) I want to associate with **"like-minded" people**, who, synergistically with me, want the best for others.

WHAT I DON'T WANT

A) I don't want the ball and chain of a retail establishment and its time demands.
B) I don't want high expenses, increasing costs and surprise cash outlays.
C) I don't want my ambitions, drive, originality, or abilities to get eaten up by un-ambitious people—the parasites of enterprise.
D) I don't want to net 10%, with 90% going to operation costs—In fact I want to net the 90%.
E) I don't want all the normal expense of a business—rent, insurance, licenses, registrations, Research and Development, employees, etc.
F) I don't want to have to buy, lease or take care of expensive office equipment.
G) I don't want a big business, with big-time headaches.
H) I don't want large start up costs for me or others, and huge expenditures to grow the business.
I) I don't want costly entanglements with agreements, contracts and messy relationships.
J) I don't want ongoing commitments with no exit strategies planned.
K) I don't want to live for the business, but have the business live for me—providing a nice life style.
L) I don't want to be around people who are just there for the next paycheck, and could care less about the enterprise.

"The greatest things ever done on earth have been done
by little and little—little agents, little persons,
little things, by every one doing his own work,
filling his own sphere, holding his own
post, and saying 'Lord, what wilt thou have me to do?'"

~Thomas Guthrie

CHAPTER THREE
COVERED CALL CLASSICS

Over the years I've written extensively on the covered call cash flow strategy. The following is taken from "Wade Cook's Stock Picking Handbook", pp.153-160. Because my last name is 'Cook', I went into the kitchen and explained writing covered calls as a cooking recipe.

Most people like frosting, obviously some more than others, as we can tell by looking at the waistlines of Americans. The following recipe is not about the cake but about the *icing on the cake*. You know from your life experiences that many cakes have really good frosting. Sometimes it is almost as thick as the cake underneath. Other times frosting is very skimpy, barely covering the cake.

When a cake is in the process of being served, it's interesting to watch how some people say they want a corner piece so they can get more frosting, and others want a center piece with frosting only on the top of the cake and not on the sides.

This strategy is about adding power to an existing strategy. It is a wonderful strategy, which, once mastered, will actually bring cash into your account. It is called Writing Covered Calls. It is designed to add money to your asset base. It is a perfect strategy for bailing yourself out of a bad stock situation. It can be done monthly or longer term. It can be adjusted to fit your lifestyle and your trading style. You can be as busy as you want, or as passive as you want.

Cooking Utensils:
There are three components for making this frosting.

1) We need to add "open position" to our trading utensils; in this case, it's a selling strategy. Anytime the word "write" is utilized in the stock market, it means to "sell." To write a call means to *sell* a call option. To write a put means to *sell* a put option. In this

case we are going to sell a call option, thereby generating cash into our account against the stock position we own. By selling, we open a position.

If we own 600 shares of a stock we have the right to sell six call option contracts against that position. In short, this would give a purchaser of these call options the right to buy our stock away from us at a set price. We use the word "covered" because we actually own the stock. We agree to sell our 600 shares at a certain price. We will sell them, or get "called out" if the stock is at or above the strike price on the expiration date—the third Friday of the specified month. We could get called out early, but this rarely happens. Boo Hoo…Usually, we write covered calls to actually sell our stock; by getting called out before the expiration date, we have rushed our profits to the "now" position and we have cash to do other deals.

2) In most situations we need an underlying stock. We could do this in a "naked" position—meaning that we do not own the stock, but we'll cover that strategy another time. You could also do a variation of this strategy with another call option as the underlying investment and create something called a bull call spread; we'll save that for another lesson as well. (See *Safety First Investing*)

We should not forget any of the components of our discussion on buying and owning good stocks. We should check the fundamentals, the technicals and the OMFs (Other Motivating Factors) such as news, to see that our underlying investment is solid. We want the company to have a good story line—meaning, every likelihood the stock will continue to move up. If you own stocks and you think they are going to move down, you should use some of the repair kit strategies, as in stop loss orders and buying puts to protect the downside. In short, you write covered calls when you are happy to own the underlying stock investment.

As I have mentioned in other chapters of other books on Writing Covered Calls, the most important underlying question—the foundation of this process—is to ask a question upon which all decisions will be based. That question is this: "Do I want to get called out?" ("Called out" means to sell the stock.) Look at the underlying stock. If the stock is weak and not showing signs of recovery, you may want to go ahead and sell the stock outright and not write a covered call. If the stock is weak but showing signs of recovery you may want to sell a slightly in-the-money call or slightly out-of-the-money call—again, depending on the answer to the above question.

If you want to keep the stock for writing covered calls for several months then you would sell an out-of-the-money call. For example if we own a $28 stock, we would sell the $30 call, or even the $35 call. If you don't care whether you sell the stock or not then you could write a slightly in-the-money or slightly out-of-the-money call option and let it ride until expiration, then wait and see if you are called out or not. That final resolution will be determined by where the stock is compared to the strike price on the expiration date. I bring this up again because you will not be able to choose which of these ingredients you are going to put into this frosting until you know whether you want to keep owning the stock or not. All of your decisions rely upon the answer to this question.

3) Call option. We should have a good working knowledge of what makes up the pricing model of a call option. When we are in the business of selling, we should try to sell for the highest price possible. In writing an option we are probably going to sell it for the price at the "BID." Even though it is the market price for that snapshot in time, we do not have to sell it at exactly that price. We can put in an order to sell the call option for any price we think we can get.

When we sell a call option, we are basically taking on an obligation. We should be paid well for taking on that obligation, which is to deliver the stock or sell the stock at a set price. Like all options, these positions have an expiration date. Our position will be considered "open" until the stock is either called away from us early, which means we have sold it, or until we arrive at the expiration date. All options expire (have no time value) on their expiration date.

When we own stock, we own the future of the stock—regardless of what earnings and other factors may do to the price of the stock. By selling the call option against the stock, (the option premium), we have given away the "upside" potential of the stock. We have sold away everything above the strike price.

If we own a $28 stock, and sell the $30 call option for .75¢, we will take in $75 for each contract. Let's once again say we have 600 shares of the stock, which, at six contracts at $75 each, will generate $450. The $450 will hit our account in one day, but the position could remain open until the expiration date. If the stock goes up to $31 or $32, and if we have not closed out the position, we will not participate in anything above $30. But, we will participate in anything *up to* $30. If the stock is at $28 and it goes to $32, then on the expiration date we will get called out at $30. This means we also make another $2 per share. Multiplied by our 600 shares, we wind up with another $1,200, in addition to our $450 for selling the calls.

Before the expiration date, we can always buy back the call option. For example, the stock has risen to $29.75, time has elapsed, and the expiration date is imminent. There is virtually little time value left in the premium as the option is worth .35¢ cents. We have a couple of choices: 1) We can just leave it alone. The stock will either stay below $30 or go above $30. We are willing to keep the stock or have it purchased away from us: 2) We could buy back the call position which would neutralize, or end, the open position.

Let's say the $30 call option is now worth .35¢—remember it is only a quarter out-of-the-money. You must ask yourself "Why?" We might be able to sell the $30 call option for the next month out for $2.50. This would generate $1,500 cash into our account. We have kept the same strike price (purchasing back the original option), but we have moved the expiration date one month into the future by selling the next month out.

Another scenario would be the $35 call option. It's going for .75¢. We take in .75¢, multiplied by 6 contracts (600 shares), and we generate another $450. It seems almost like extra busy work, but just think: we have spent $210 (.35¢ x 6 contracts) and we have generated another $450 cash into our account. One good thing is that we have moved up $5 on the strike price. If the stock were to continue to rise and we were to get called out at $35 that could generate another $5 multiplied by 600 shares, or $3,000 into the account. Plus, the $1200 from $28 to $30 as mentioned before.

One of the reasons I like writing covered calls is because of the "buy back" feature, which always allows us to regain control of our money. You can sell away the upside of a stock, and then buy it back. Many of my students do this two or three times a month. In short, they sell the call option on a rise, buy it back on a dip, and then on the next rise in the stock they sell the call option again. They keep the same stock and try to use it multiple times for generating income into their accounts. The most I have ever done this has been two times in one month. It is simply because I am too busy to monitor my accounts in such an extreme manner. Many of my students do better than me as they have more time to do this extra homework.

Ingredients For The Cake:

The main point is that these ingredients are going to be blended with the utensils. This frosting is going to become the cake, and the cake is going to become the frosting to a certain extent. The covered call we are going to write to generate income is going to be married to the stock position. Therefore the quality of the "derivative" is going to be based on the quality of the underlying investment. If you have a high quality investment, one that you have purchased after doing much homework, then your ability to make money in writing covered calls will be effectively enhanced. Don't try to get a really great tasting cake from really bad ingredients.

We need a good market place to operate in. If the kitchen is all messy and dirty and causes an inability to properly use the ingredients, we may want to sit it out until the kitchen is cleaned up. The stock market can also become very sloppy. It can be in a down-trending mode, and nothing we do seems to work. I have had experiences like this over the years, and it is hard to make quality trades in a less than quality market place.

Baking Instructions:
As in all option positions, the baking instructions and time constraints will be in accordance with the underlying stock.

Timing:

1) Usually we write a covered call for around three to four weeks out. This means that at the end of each expiration date, the week after the third Friday of the month, we will write the next month out covered call. We try to pick up (sell) as much time as we can.

2) We may not want to sell the call at that time if the stock is on a dip. A Wade Cook Market Maxim that will make this strategy work is this: "buy the stock on a dip (weakness) and sell the option on strength." If we think the stock is going to rise in the near term we may want to wait to sell the call option. Please note: you can put in an order to sell an option that is currently at a dollar for $2 by placing a GTC order, or "Good Till Canceled."

3) You can also do a buy/write and get one trade a little cheaper. A buy/write happens when you buy the stock and sell the calls simultaneously.

4) If we find that we have more time to monitor the position, we may be able to rapidly sell the call, and buy the call back on the next dip

in the stock, a week or ten days later, and then sell the call option once again on the next rise. I alluded to this before. It is similar to doing a rolling stock but doing it as a rolling covered call. This could be done multiple times—again, based on your dedication and the amount of time you have to monitor the position.

5) We could also do a *L.O.C.C.* (Large Option Covered Call). In this type of transaction we would sell the call option for 5 or 7 months into the future. We hope to get called out, and by doing so, generate a huge premium—sometimes 80% to 100% of margin amount we use to purchase the stock. I have written extensively on this topic in *Free Stocks: How to Get the Stock Market to Pay for Your Stocks.* I think this book is especially applicable to people who are very busy with their businesses or careers.

If we own a down-trending stock, or if we are trading in a weak or down-trending market, the following strategy may help. We have a stock we do not want to sell. We want to wait for it to turn around. One way to trade is to sell an "in-the-money" call. Let's go back to our $28 stock. It has dipped from $35 but we don't necessarily want to sell it. It has not shown signs of recovery. In fact it could continue to go down. We could "pre-capture" the profits right now. We could sell the $25 call. The stock is at $28 and the $25 call is going for $5.50. Now if the stock dips down to $26 we would have pre-captured the larger premium generating more cash into the account than by selling the $30 call option. In this case we would get called out at $25. Again we can still buy back the $25 call as we near the expiration date, end the position, and then sell the $25 call for a further out month. If the stock drops to $24 we would not get called out. We would still own the stock. But look at this: the stock has dropped from $28 to $24, a four-dollar drop. We have picked up $5.50. We still gained $1.50, in spite of a drop in the stock. This speaks to the fact that there are "stock repair kit" methods to recover from a down trending stock.

Now with the stock at $24, we can make a host of new decisions. We can sell the $25 calls, or the $22.50 calls for the next month. Do we take in a bigger premium now on a lower strike price or a lower premium on a higher strike price, hoping that the stock will go up? The point is that we are back in control of the decision-making process.

How To Eat:
This whole section has not been so much about market timing but about length of timing for writing a covered call. Once you get a good understanding of how call option premiums work, and specifically how the option price deteriorates with the passage of time, you will be able to make many wise decisions. This strategy is designed to work on a variety of cakes. For example, you might have some of the following:

1) You have a rolling stock going between $6 and $8. While it is moving towards $8 you may find it advantageous to sell the $7.50 call and put some extra cash into your account right now.

2) You may have purchased a "slammed" stock which has gone from $18 down to $12 and you are waiting for it to bounce, but it hasn't quite bounced in the time period you wanted it to. You can sell the $10 calls or the $12.50 calls and generate cash while you are waiting for the stock to bounce higher.

3) You could have your semester investor type stock that you are holding for 2 or 3 years, but from time to time you could use those right term hold stocks for writing covered calls for generating extra income.

The point is that many stocks serve many purposes. One of my suggestions at many of my seminars has been to pick your top 10 or 20 stocks. Just like the top 20 in a rock-n-roll list of songs, you have your top 20 in stock-n-roll. You can get good at 20 stocks. You can understand the basic mission of the company: you can learn important dates of the company, like earnings reports and other news types events: you can notice patterns and chart certain stocks. You can even memorize support and resistance levels. Most human minds cannot do this with hundreds or thousands of stocks. I know a lot of people try to do this with their computers and I wish them well. I have found that in my busy life I do most of my trades on the phone to and from basketball and while I am out running errands. I cannot look at a computer screen, or even printed out charts. I have to do my investing through the eyes and ears of other people. This has caused me to limit the volume of stocks I am trading; again, I limit the amount so I can become an expert on a few stocks. I do not want to be guilty of "jack of all trades and master of none." I suggest you consider the same. Get to be an expert on a few stocks—-stocks you like, and not burden your mind with so much clutter that you have a hard time keeping track of the stocks in your portfolio or stocks you want to trade.

Covered calls are a workhorse, the frosting that will make everything taste better. You can use it all of the time, and once you get good at it, I will suggest to you now that it will become a strategy that will work for you in good times and bad times and one that will help you generate more cash and build up your assets in your stock market portfolio.

WRITING COVERED CALLS

> *"I wrote a covered call on RMFD, stock went down just after I sold the call. I bought my position back that same day, the stock went up the next day. I sold the stock and made approximately $1,000 on the option and sale of the stock—this was a two day deal."*
>
> *-Allen R., NC*

> *"Cash in was $2,000, profit was $1,750. That is a 87.5% return in 10 days."*
>
> *-Alton C., FL*

> *"I purchased SCIO stock 2 weeks ago at 19.50. I sold the calls for 4.75 or $1,425. I had 150 shares on margin. If I get called out at 20.00 I have a $1,575 return on a $3,000 investment for a 50% return in 1 month."*
>
> *-Benjamin C., UT*

"Covered call CPWR 9.60 bought on dip. Wait to sell calls at 1.45 on 40 contracts made $5,800 on $23,600."

-Bill B., MI

"November 29, 2001 I bought 2 contracts of the Jan 30 calls on ISSX on news that it was being added to S & P mid-days. It was at 29.06 on November 30. I got out with a $1.50 profit, which was a 17% return overnight! Very exciting trade."

-Christa K., B.C.

YOUR NEW INCOME MACHINE

In honor of Wade Cook's cab—Number 22—we've provided 22 reasons why you need covered calls. It's about the "meter-drop", making steady income and making it in bite-size pieces.

1) Every market provides opportunities for income—some better, some worse—but there is never a time you can't sell options.
2) Covered Call Writing makes it possible to choose your level of risk—choose steady stocks or do more fluctuating types—you're in control.
3) Writing Covered Calls is available to everyone—even now—millions of Americans are leaving billions of dollars on the table.
4) Selling Calls puts market forces to work for you, not against you, i.e., time and implied volatility (fluffy premiums).
5) You can do Writing Covered Calls as an amateur with even limited skills and produce sensational profits.
6) Writing Covered Calls is a powerful "assets producing income" strategy, so you can live a lifestyle of your choosing.
7) It's easy to paper-trade and develop skills, before you put your real money to work.
8) Writing Covered Calls allows you to pull out cash or leave it alone to purchase more stocks and produce even more income.
9) Skills for Writing Covered Calls can be developed, expanded and enhanced. You easily move from once a month income to two and five times a month income.
10) Writing Covered Calls allows you to calculate your profits (rate of return) before you enter the trade. You won't get millionaire rich, but you'll get "millionaire cash flow rich."
11) Writing Covered Calls gives you your profits first. You get "Paid to Trade". These profits are certain. Writing Covered Calls puts the emphasis on selling—like all other businesses. The stock market truly becomes a business—your own cash flow machine.
12) If you're really busy, you can write calls four to seven months out (LOCC—Large Option Covered Calls) and generate huge profits.

13) Writing Covered Calls gives you a speedy way to fix broken stocks. Instead of being a victim, you have a way to pound profits back into your account.
14) Writing Covered Calls is all about making "correctable decisions", not just correct decisions. As stocks move up or down, you can buy-back and sell again to make more money.
15) You can protect against downside stock moves with stop losses and puts. However, the same stock at $7.50, $12.50 or $17.50 (up or down) still produces monthly income.
16) Selling calls can de done wherever you are: at home, on vacation, or during coffee breaks.
17) Money ($2,000 to $10,000) can be worked in less than five hours a month.
18) It's functionally easy to conduct the investment and trade. It can be done in 30 seconds to one minute on a cell phone—at a red light.
19) Writing Covered Call provides steady income on a monthly basis.
20) Writing Covered Calls makes it possible to quit your job faster and better than you've ever thought possible.
21) You can write covered calls in an IRA or pension account with no current tax on the profits. These profits grow exponentially.
22) And best of all, Wade Cook is in the trenches, doing the deals and leading the way. You want an income machine, he's provided an education machine to help you.

WRITING COVERED CALLS, your new RIG—Repetitive Income Generator

The staff at Liberty Network

CHAPTER FOUR
GETTING YOU THROUGH THE COVERED CALL LEARNING CURVE:
Let's Do Some Deals

ARE YOU AN INVESTOR OR TRADER?

Let's discuss whether you are an investor or a trader. There is a world of difference between the two. An investor would be considered a "right-term" person. A trader is someone who is using the stock market for a more immediate reward. In real estate I purchased some rental properties to hold for four to ten years. But I made bigger money, especially at the beginning of my career, in short term plays. By that I mean; buying a house on Monday and fixing it by Tuesday or Wednesday, putting it up for sale on Thursday, and hopefully closing by the next Monday or Tuesday. I became very good at this by only purchasing properties that I could turn over quickly.

In the stock market there is a similar method. You look for short-term trades to generate income. This is a business type income. I have often said on radio and TV shows that we need to treat the stock market like a business. If you do so, you will be considered a "trader." One side benefit is that all the expenses of trading would be expensed out or tax deductible if you meet the requirements. Another potential side benefit would be that you would hopefully make enough money with short-term trades (meaning three-day to three-month trades) to pay your bills each month and have enough to take home as well as enough to put into slightly longer "right-term" trades, or move away from the market to real estate, oil, or other investments.

Yes you can be an investor and a trader at the same time. You could dedicate part of your money to each enterprise. One is a very active enterprise, requiring an active involvement; the other requires a passive involvement. Nevertheless each one requires its own level of expertise;

each type requires a certain amount of homework and dedication to know the investments you are holding for each purpose.

"Buy and Hold" *can* work if given 30 years or more, but I feel that there is such a better way. Yes, position trading is more work, but the results are definitely worth the effort. The hold period must be appropriate. It must fit your risk tolerance, your own particular stage in life and your own cash flow needs. You can get your money to work harder as you learn to deploy money the way you would in any other business. Trading is a business—a business that can support your family. All you have to do is change your expectation level and learn how to "work" your money better. The past correction in the marketplace, seen as risky by some, provided great opportunities for others. It provides investment opportunities, as well as trading opportunities.

These two strategies are symbiotic. As you develop skills as a trader you will learn to choose better investments. Conversely, the study and search for good investments will net many trading opportunities. To get good at both methods we need to find, study, practice and work each formula and then find stocks or options to fit the formula.

WHAT IS MY JOB?

> *"The Highest Function of the teacher consists not so much in imparting knowledge as in stimulating the pupil in its love and pursuit."*
>
> ~Henri Frederic Amiel

My life has been most interesting. I take my life as an educator very seriously. Here's an interesting quote, *"For every person wishing to teach, there are thirty not wanting to be taught." ~ W.C. Sellar.* I hope you're not one of the thirty. In fact it speaks volumes to the kind of person you are that you're reading this book and sticking with it.

Good things lie ahead for you. I personally believe God is wonderful. I know he has a plan for us:

"For I know the thoughts that I think toward you, saith the Lord, Thoughts of peace, and not of evil, to give you an expected end."
~Jeremiah 29:11

I know He is great and has great things in store for us. And yet so many of us get bogged down in the mundane things in life and don't see the bigger and greater picture. I've often said, "*Our purpose in life should be to build a life of purpose.*" This is based on a quotation by Woodrow Wilson, our 28th President.

"You are not here merely to make a living. You are here to enable the world to live more amply, with greater vision, with a finer spirit of hope and achievement. You are here to enrich the world, but will lessen yourself if you forget the errand."

Since I was a young man I've known I wanted to work with people and with money. An early church leader told me that he saw me as a teacher. Today, my career is my hobby and my hobby is my career. I have a passion to help people live more fully, more richly. Money isn't everything, but it sure can do a lot of good for other people. Most people attracted to my seminars realize that making money is work. It takes skills and perseverance.

"*Studies indicate that the one quality all successful people have is persistence. They're willing to spend more time accomplishing a task and to persevere in the face of many difficult odds. There's a very positive relationship between people's ability to accomplish any task and the time they're willing to spend on it."*

~ Dr. Joyce Brothers

What does all this mean to you? Well know this, I only teach what I do. You see, most of the financial professionals tell you, "Hey Americans, you're not smart enough to understand stocks and bonds. We have the tools and the intelligence. Give your money to us and we'll manage it for you." Then along comes Wade Cook and says, "Wait Americans. You are smart enough. I'll lead the way—figure out what the truly wealthy do and how the great traders and investors act—and share it with you. I'll try and test these strategies and formulas, and with my cab driving experience as a background, I'll show it to you. Let's walk down this road together." You see, I'm a student first, an educator second. So before you buy stocks and bonds, take stock in knowledge and bond with us.

So, let's see if you get it. Do you understand the basics of covered call writing?

Check out American Pharmaceutical (APPX). The stock is at $42.15. Even up in this range there are $42.50 strike prices, as well as $40 and $45 calls. Many heavily traded stocks defy the old rules and have interim strike prices.

The $42.50 calls out seven weeks are going for $2.00. This is a more expensive stock, so in order to diversify our small portfolio, let's buy 400 shares. 400 times $42.15 is $16,860. Fifty percent margin would be $8,430. Again our choice would be to sell now or wait. Each has an advantage. We're so busy we just decide to sell the $42.50 calls now. 400 shares allow us to sell four contracts at $2.00, and take in $800. If we get called out we'd make another $140. ($42.50 - $42.15 = .35 x 400 = $140).

That would bring our profit to $940. Measure it out. $800 (or $940) with $8,430 tied up. Even on the full amount of $16,860, it's not bad. By the way, that would be the cash return in an Individual Retirement Account. You can't do margin investing in an IRA.

Oh, you ask, "What about the $40 calls?" OK, let's go there. This would be an in-the-money call. We'd pick up more cash now, but by selling the stock for $40, we'd lose $2.15 times 400 shares. The $40 calls are a nice $3.40. We'd take in $1,360 ($3.40 x 400), but have to give back $860. Our net would be $500. Less overall profits, but more certainty. Pretty darn good either way.

Two points:

1. If you want to keep the stock and let it ride, sell the $42.50 calls.
2. If you think the stock has peaked in the short term, and if you want to do multiple "double-dipping" type trades, sell the $40 calls. As the stock backs off, you quickly buy back the option, sell on the next rise, buy it back again—lather, rinse, repeat.

Okay, your first test:

1. Can you watch a financial show on TV and list four to five stocks you know?
2. Can you check out the Q's—The NASDAQ 100 (Ticker QQQQ) and find a few stocks you know?
3. Can you check a chart or two to see if a stock is on a dip or at a high?

Every stock site I know of has charts. We don't need to be a chartist to observe, connect the dots, and buy at a good time.

4. Can you call your broker and get an option price (A) this month and next month, and (B) One strike price below and one strike price above the current strike price?
5. Can you . . . ask the all important question: "Do I want to sell the stock, or not?"
6. Think. Pencil it out. If I do this, then I'll make this much. If I do that, then I'll make that much more later.

Remember, you can calculate your certain profits now. What you can't calculate is what you'll do if the stock goes down or if it goes up (say, way up) above the strike price. We'll deal with each of these later, but for now—how does it look? Try it. Make the call. Okay, here's a few to check out: JNPR, INTC, JBLU, NOK, BRCM, XLNX, CSCO and MSFT. Measure your risk reward ratio. Is it right for you?

Back to My Job. I've got to convince you that (A) <u>You</u> can do it, (B) You can do it <u>now</u> in this market, and (C) you can do it <u>where you are</u>—your car, your back bedroom, or on your lunch break.

This is a medium to great market for writing covered calls. There is just not that much volatility, so call prices are not too high. This market is still a bit "range-bound". As the market picks up, option prices will expand and we'll make more. We used to get 20% to 30% a month. Today we have to do multiple trades to get those cash returns.

I firmly believe experiential learning is the best, most valuable way of progressing. Learn and earn is a great way to proceed. With that in mind, let's proceed.

QUESTION: WHAT STOCKS CAN I WATCH?

Well, how about the most watched batch of stocks in the world—The DOW. This is the DJIA, or Dow Jones Industrial Average. It includes a grouping of stocks that represent a wide spectrum of American business. It also now includes a few NASDAQ stocks, not just stocks from the New York Stock Exchange.

Our study will be simple. We'll take the current price of the stock and a one month out option. We'll check two strike prices—one below and one above the stock price.

Here's an interesting observation: You'll be able to use hindsight and check out how these stocks have done. Up or down—your viewpoint will be from an interesting perspective. It should help you choose better stocks for the future.

After the list is given, I'll put in my two cents worth. I'll pick a few for comments; maybe even do a few trades. First, most of these won't work—at least not for 10% plus monthly returns. Why? They don't move enough and therefore the option premiums will be somewhat smaller. You might think, "Wow, cheap options—I should buy some of these." Yes, maybe, but cheap does not mean good. They are definitely not safe. Inexpensive options simply means the option market makers do not think the stock will move much. To make money in buying calls and puts, the stock has to move in the direction you desire, and move quickly, or you will lose.

Let me introduce you to No.R.M. trades. This is a new way to look at covered calls. NoRM stands for No Required Movement. Remember stocks move up, down or sideways. How would it be to do the trade and then not have to worry? You've made your money! Be cool and go to a movie.

"With ordinary talent and extraordinary perseverance, all things are attainable."
~Thomas Fowell Buxton

There is no happiness in mediocrity. There is happiness in growth, in new challenges—in creating something. Malcolm Forbes said, *"No success is ever accomplished by a reasonable man."*

J. Paul Getty, the famous billionaire said, "*No one can possibly achieve any real and lasting success or "get rich" in business by being a conformist."*

Company Name	Ticker	Stock Price	Strike Below	Option Price (Bid)	Strike Above	**Option Price (Bid)**
Alcoa	AA	27.31	25	2.50	27.50	.70
American Express	AXP	54.45	50	4.60	55	.80
American Int'l. Grp.	AIG	54.93	50	5.20	65	1.40
Boeing	BA	64.45	60	4.90	65	1.40
Caterpillar	CAT	96.10	95	3.30	100	1.10
Citigroup	C	47.83	47.50	1.10	50	.10
Coca Cola	KO	43.91	42.50	1.45	45	.20
Dupont	DD	46.49	45	2.00	47.50	.55
Pfizer	PFE	27.71	27.50	.80	30	.05
Exxon Mobil	XOM	51.15	55	2.95	60	.50
General Electric	GE	36.89	35	2.00	37.50	.30
General Motors	GM	31.78	30	2.35	32.50	1.00
Hewlett-Packard	HPQ	22.42	20	2.45	22.50	.50

Home Depot	HD	39.82	37.50	2.65	40	.90
Honeywell	HON	36.22	35	1.70	37.50	.40
Int. Business Mach	IBM	74.75	70	5.40	75	1.80
Intel	INTC	27.05	25	2.25	27.50	.60
Verizon	VZ	35.03	35	.60	37.50	.00
Johnson&Johnson	JNJ	66.34	65	2.05	70	.15
McDonalds	MCD	29.95	27.50	2.00	30	.45
Microsoft	MSFT	25.45	25	.80	27.50	.05
Merck	MRK	31.68	30	2.10	32.50	.50
MN Mining & Mfg	MMM	76.66	75	2.75	80	.50
Disney	DIS	27.45	25	2.55	27.50	.55
JP Morgan	JPM	35.72	35	1.10	37.50	.10
Altria(Philip Morris)	MO	68.71	65	4.00	70	1.15
Proctor Gamble	PG	55.40	55	1.25	60	.05
SBC Comm.	SBC	23.51	22.50	1.05	25	.00
United Technology	UTX	106.50	105	3.30	110	.95
Walmart	WMT	47.46	45	2.75	47.50	.90

I'm now staring at the page of DJIA 30 stocks. These stocks represent a broad swath of United States businesses. You're looking at Americana in action.

I've made many comments over the past while about this market being "range bound". It's fenced in. There are some natural and some mental barriers holding the market up—and holding the market back. A few years ago there were giant 300 and 400 point 2-3 day swings. Now that is a rarity. Sometimes it takes weeks for the market to move up a few hundred points. And weeks for it to move back down. It's always in motion, its motion is just not overly erratic.

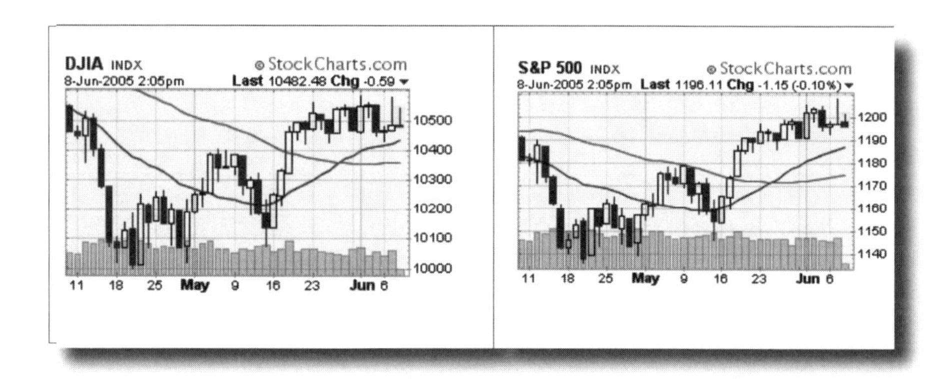

Small movements cause option prices to shrink. This book is not about buying options and I haven't spent much time on option prices. What is it that makes up the option price? Let's explore this, and then get back to the DOW and see how the information applies.

Option market makers are in the business of making money, and sadly this means in most instances that someone has to lose. They have many ways to drive stocks up a little and down a little. They use computer program models to help set prices. If they say an option is $1.50, just what comprises the $1.50? Simply put, they're going to sell the option for what someone will pay for it. Another stock at a similar price might have the same strike price option going for $2.75, another one is 75 cents. Why the difference? Because somebody will pay more for certain options.

The two biggest components of the option premium are the time value—the time to expiration, and the "speculative value"—or more commonly said, "implied volatility". The time to expiration is a real number, but it is measurable because, day by day, time goes away. We call this deterioration of the premium. You might own a call option, thinking a stock will go up, and it does. It goes up like you thought, but it's taking too long. The option premium goes down because there isn't that much time left. Time works against you. Time is not your friend.

The "implied volatility" portion of the option is where the fun begins. If a market maker (and the whole market for that matter) thinks a stock is going to zoom—say go up $30 in the next year—the options will be very expensive. The $50 call option out a few months is $8. It's really expensive. To control 1,000 shares, the pricc would bc $8,000. That's a lot.

Covered call writers should learn this well. If you owned this stock and were to sell the $50 calls, realizing you're selling away everything over $50, wouldn't you want to get paid well? I think so. However if you have a $50 stock that's not going anywhere, the $50 strike price options for the same month could be $1, not $8. Summary, what will someone pay? That determines the price of the options.

Let's get back to the DOW 30:

1. Alcoa. $31,400 to buy 1,000 shares. $15,700 on margin. You could sell the $32.50 calls for $450. You would make another $1,100 if the stock goes above $32.50 and you get called out. Is this an okay return, or should you shop around?
2. Look at Caterpillar. The $100 calls are 45 cents. You'd take in $450 but have put up $95,670 to buy 1,000 shares of stock. Half of that on margin.
3. Check out GE. There is virtually no "time value" in the premium. The stock is $37; the $35 calls are at $2. It's all in-the-money.
4. You could generate $750 on IBM by selling the $100 calls and pick up another $3,000 or so if you were called out at $100. Cost? A lot. You don't have to buy 100 shares—you could buy 200 or 400 shares and sell two or four contracts. 1,000 shares would cost about $97,000. Even on margin that would be $48,500. Too much tied up for my blood. $750 is not enough. Yes, the $3,000 extra capital gain would be nice, but that isn't certain money.
5. Others: Merck is not bad. Intel is okay. HPQ provides a little.

Check them all out if you like. It's good homework. However, for me, there are better deals elsewhere. Already in this book we've made over $750 (like the IBM option), but on $5,000 into the stock (unlike the IBM stock at $97,000).

One last point. As the market heats up, option volatility will also pick up. If we can get good at covered call writing in this range-bound marketplace, we will do so much better with all of these improvements. The DJIA 30 stocks usually do not provide large premiums. We'll have to look at more volatile stocks. One thing is certain: STOCK PRICES FLUCTUATE. We need stocks that move up and down $1 to $3 every one to three days.

10-4 GOOD BUDDY

Many attendees of my seminars, responding to my radio interviews and buying my books usually have around $5,000 to $30,000 to trade. I believe in diversification, but of a different stripe than most Wall Street bigwigs. I teach formula diversification. Don't put all your eggs in one basket. $30,000 would only buy 1000 shares of a $30 stock, non-margin. My suggestion is to take $30,000 and put it into four to six trades. To keep my life simple, I buy 1000 shares of $5 to $25 stocks and 400 shares of $25, $35, or $50 stocks. For Example:

NFLX	1000 x 16 = $16,000 or $8,000 on margin
TIVO	1000 x 5.80 = $5,800 or $2900 on margin
NANO	1000 x 11 = $11,000 or $5500 on margin
RMBS	400 x 14 = $5600 or $2800 on margin
QCOM	400 x 36 = $14,400 or $7,200 on margin
SIRI	1000 x 5.90 =$5900 or $2950 on margin
	Total on Margin $39,350

Now, here's an interesting point. These stocks, used for writing covered calls, produce about $4,600 in extra cash income. The brokerage computer just recognizes this as cash. If you do nothing it will just lower your margin requirement. However, you could take it out to live on. You could buy more stock ($9000 more) and sell another call for $1,000. And on and on.

My thoughts are to keep this new money around. Why? You might have a margin call or requirement if a stock dips. Also, if you want to gear up and buy back the call to resell at a higher price, you'll need some cash on hand to do so.

HERE ARE SOME EXAMPLES FROM T.S.T (Trading Skills and Techniques):

"On XXIA I got $1.05 on selling the May $17.50 Calls. It is pretty cool, in a way because, about three weeks ago when I bought the stock, I sold the May $17.50 Calls for $1.45, bought them back a few days later at .35. So I made $1100 on this trade, and I just sold them again today for $1.05, so it is another $1,050 profit."

"I just bought back the April $16 calls on AMD for .70¢ and put in an order to sell the May $17 calls for .95¢, I could sell the May $16 calls for $1.10 and make .15¢ more. Right now the $17 calls are .65¢ x. 75¢ so with a down market I might have to wait until tomorrow or another up tick day to be able to get hit on that."

Let's review:

1. I've already captured the profits on this trade. I sold the call last week. The stock is Rambus (RMBS). It was around $24. I sold the next month out calls for $3.20. I have 400 shares. I sold four contracts of the January $25 calls and took in $1,280. I had a standing order to buy them back at $1.40. That happened this morning before I got out of bed. The cost was $560. My net is $720.
2. I had previously sold the December $25 calls for $1.80, or $620 and bought them back for 80 cents or $320, netting $300.
3. I also bought 200 more shares today at $21.88. Now I have 600 shares. The stock is back up to $22.20. I could have purchased the 200 shares for $20.90. I'm not into the inane strategy of "dollar cost averaging." I'm into buying on dips—and hopefully as the stock price is moving back up.
4. I have an order in to sell the January calls ($25 strike price) on my 600 shares for $2.55.

5. This all took about ten minutes of my time.
6. Watch me do this on T.S.T.™ (Trading Skills and Techniques) at www.wadecook.org. Hopefully I can do two to three more trades. I still have four weeks to go.
7. Remember, it's about cash flow. I can make just as much with the stock at $22 as I can with the stock at $25. I might change the order and sell the $22.50 call. It's going for $2.20. I would take in $1,320 (600 x $2.20 = $1,320)

A few days later I sold the $22.50 calls on RMBS for $1.95. 600 shares times $1.95 is $1,170. This is the third trade in three weeks.

Recap:		
Recap:	1st sell and Buy Back	= $300
	2nd sell and Buy Back	= $720
	3rd sell	= $1170 (buy back pending)

This totals $2,170 in extra cash. It is found money. I still plan on doing one to two more sell and buy backs—and still own the stock and start writing the February calls. In baseball we call this manufacturing runs. It's working the trade for multiple hits in the ol' cash flow ball park.

Cheer if it goes up, cheer if it goes down. It's a winning strategy. Talk about winning the complete game, read on to an edited transcription of a live seminar I taught. I hope this helps you focus in on what it takes for you to win.

CHAPTER FIVE
WHAT MAKES STOCK GO UP AND DOWN IN PRICE

FEAR AND GREED
Virtually every movement in the stock market is created by one of two human emotions: fear or greed. This aspect of stock market movement cannot be overemphasized.

Remember, when you buy a company you are buying it for "fear" or "greed" purposes. If you really believe a company has the potential for making a lot of money, your purchase would fall under the greed category. Conversely, you sell because of fear. Yes, you've been greedy; your stock is up, so you sell before it goes back down. In short, fear and/or greed is/are the underlying emotions of all stock movements.

THE LAW OF SUPPLY AND DEMAND
I was getting ready to go play basketball and my young son of 14, just about 15, came in to see me while my wife and I were talking. We were discussing some reports I had just read about the up-trending market, of which I have just written a new book. He said to me, "Dad, what makes stocks go up?" We only had a few minutes to talk so I basically told him that stocks go up and down because of the law of supply and demand.

I continued briefly that there are only so many shares of stock in any one company, and when there are many people who want that stock, the price of the stock will have the tendency to go up. Conversely, when a lot of people do not want the stock but want to sell the stock, it will have the tendency to go down. All I had time to explain was that there was a middleman, like a warehouse. In this case it would be either the Specialist on the New York Stock Exchange or the Market Maker on NASDAQ. That person is the middleman in buying and selling stocks, similar to a warehouse in buying and selling groceries. For example:

at a certain time of year if there is a big demand for oranges, and the warehouse is getting low, they could raise their price and people would be willing to pay the higher price because they want oranges. There is a demand for them. If the oranges have aged, or if nobody wanted them for whatever reason and if they were sitting there not selling, then the warehouseman could lower the price in order to create a price level where people would want to finally buy.

This law of supply and demand, while simplistic, still answers most of what goes on in the marketplace everyday. As a matter of fact, to make it even more simplistic, let me share with you what my stockbroker frequently tells me. I know that he is very busy and when I call him about the market and/or a particular stock and it is up to $30, I usually ask the question "Well what caused that?" He is probably at that point in time typing away to get the stories or related information about the stock so he can give me a good answer. But while he is doing this he has this cute little answer he gives in a non-committal way. He says "More buyers than sellers." Within that simple statement are deep implications. Conversely when stocks go down, he answers, "More sellers than buyers."

EARNINGS

Before we look at historically low P/Es formed in the marketplace right now, we first should discuss earnings and earnings per share, or P/E. The earnings of a company are its bottom line—they are the profits (after taking out dividends to shareholders of any preferred stock and after taxes).

To figure the earnings per share, we take the number of shares outstanding and divide it into earnings—hence we get earnings per share. Earnings are very important and are that which the company uses for dividend payouts, for investment in growth, for excess debt reduction. This figure is most often used by lending institutions for calculation of new debt paybacks.

Earnings should be from sales, and not from a one-time phenomenon, like the sale of a division, or a bad investment charge off. Many sources list earnings per share: Barron's, Investor's Business Daily, most local newspapers with financial information, and most computer on-line services.

In determining your stock purchases, you'll not only want current figures, but you'll want to know where the company has been. Does it have a history of increasing earnings? Did they increase, then slow down? We need to understand why the earnings per share are what they are.

The P/E is a very important number. I teach this from coast to coast. "When in doubt," I say, "follow earnings." Yes, the other measuring sticks are useful, but not as important as earnings. Think of it. Some companies just don't need a lot of assets to produce income. Some need a lot of assets and other forms of overhead.

The P/E is stated in terms that let us figure how much each dollar of our stock purchase is making. If the company's stock is trading at $80 and it earns $8 per share, it has a multiple of 10. If it's making $4 per share, it has a multiple, or P/E of 20; 20 times $4 equals $80. Another way would be to divide $4 into $80 and get 20, or a P/E of 20. In this case, what we're saying as investors is that we are willing to accept a 5% cash flow return (even though we may not actually receive the $4 or the $8); 5% of $80 is $4.

As I've said, P/Es are very, very important. We need to understand how to use them—and how to keep them in perspective. Let me give you a cab driver's take on this. A P/E stated as dollars just says how much you're paying for each dollar of earnings. If a company has a P/E of 42, you're paying $42 to get at one dollar of earnings. Likewise, if the P/E is 8, it means you're paying $8 to get at one dollar of earnings.

To decide if a P/E for a particular company is good, we need to: (1) pick a number we're happy with—say, "I'll buy any company with a P/E under 24," or (2) compare it to the market as a whole, or (3) compare it to stocks in the same sector, say high-tech or pharmaceuticals.

Let's look at (2), as (1) is self-explanatory. Standard and Poors has an index of 500 stocks. It's called the S&P 500. The combined P/E for these companies is in the thirties. You compare your company to this number and get a feel for how well it's doing.

You could also look at a smaller picture and compare your stock to other companies in the same business. There are so many variables in trying to get a handle on this information. One problem is that different reporting services use different time periods. For example, one newspaper may use "trailing 12 months" numbers to figure a company's P/E. It could be accurate to the last decimal, but is it appropriate to make a judgment solely based on where a company has been? Are we not buying the future—what a company will earn? Some figures are on projected earnings. If we only used this number, would that be complete—as if anybody knows what a company will actually earn? Yes, analysts (for the company or independent) can make their best guess, but they often fall short or overstate earnings.

Probably the best gauge would be to take a blend of the "trailing" and the "projected earnings." Many papers report it in some combination: say, trailing 12 and future 12 months. Many use six months back and six months future.

Because earnings are so important for good choices in selecting great stocks, let's spend a little more time on this topic.

A P/E ratio is a formula. The stock price divided by a company's earnings (the back-slash is for division). Let's say you have a stock at $30 and they announce earnings of $1 per share. We can't do the math yet. Most of these announcements are made quarterly (10Q's). In fact three times the reports are quarterly, and the year-end quarter will also produce the full year's totals. These numbers can be found in the company's 10K. Let's go ahead and work the ratio but it will not be complete. For this calculation, let's pretend the $1 is the annual earnings per share. Yes, we're pretending. $1 of earnings is then divided by the current stock price and we get an earnings ratio of 30. If the stock price is $15, the ratio would be 15. If the stock price is $60, the P/E would be 60, which is where a lot of companies on Nasdaq have their P/E ratios.

$$\frac{\$30}{\$1} = 30$$

Let's stick with the $30 stock price—a P/E of 30. Not bad, but again, not totally true. In some way we have to mentally extrapolate this $1 and make it an annual number. Could we not use the three past quarters? Yes, but we own the future, not the past. You might think, if this company makes $1 per quarter times four, there would be $4 of earnings per share. Again, this might not be accurate. Rarely does a company have even quarterly earnings. The earnings per quarter are usually different. It usually goes something like this: first quarter $1, second quarter .75 cents, third quarter .75 cents and fourth quarter .50 cents. The total for the year is $3. I'm trying to keep this simple. Now do the division.

$$\frac{\$30}{\$\ 3} = 10$$

A P/E of ten is a good number, as all the other stocks in this sector might have P/Es of 16, 18, or 28. When you read certain corporate reports, the wording can be very deceiving. You don't know if the writer is talking about trailing earnings, blended earnings, future, or forecasted earnings. But it's not that tough to get a handle on it. If you're online, using company info, or if you call your broker you will be given the trailing twelve-month earnings. And these ratios are updated instantaneously on their computer. They use the last SEC filed earnings report and a software program divides it, even as the stock price is moving. Look at the above ratio. If the stock moves to $33 (with year-end earnings at $3), then the P/E would be 11. A P/E ratio is good for determining a) if the company is making money and b) how it compares to other stocks.

A perspective: Historically, all stocks have had an *average* P/E of 15.5. Today's P/Es are a little higher. On any given day the 30 combined stocks on the DOW, or DJIA have an average P/E of 19.2, or 19.6. We usually just round off to 20. NASDAQ has averages in the mid 30's and 40's. New high-flying companies and companies which are expanding could carry P/Es of 60 to 90.

Most of you have heard of the DOT.Com Bust. (In California they sometimes refer to this as the DOTBOMB). In fact, only 9% of Internet companies failed. 91% made it in some shape or form. Even if your favorite company made it, the stock may have gone from $280 to $18. Some P/Es were at 904, or 109. I saw one at 2,200. That is the bubble that had to bust. Expectations of earnings growth were unreasonable.

You see, everything returns to the norm. If a stock is trading at a high multiple, like 904 times earnings, one of two things has to happen:

1) The earnings grow to justify this high stock price, or
2) The stock price will fall and get back in line with where it should be. What I call the "norm."

One way to be careful is to look for great companies with low P/Es. Let me give a perspective on this from a cab driver's point of view. I learned awesome lessons of life and finance as a cab driver. Those thirteen months served me well.

A few years back I used AOL's P/E as an example in my seminars. It proved an important point. This was before the merger with Time-Warner. Its P/E was 608! I used the sale of a small business netting $100,000 and how a private sale would generate $150,000 to $200,000. If this company went public, and *if* the stock traded at 20 times earnings, or a P/E of 20, it would go out at $2,000,000.

Let's look at a P/E of 608. This means investors are willing to pay $60,800,000 to get at $100,000 of earnings. It's so ridiculous; it is a wonder how these stocks got so high. It was like TULIPBULBS.com.

We as Americans paid astronomical prices for these stocks. They were way up in the stratosphere and something had to give. The bubble burst. Stock prices plummeted. Everything returns to the norm. We should learn to find solid growth, good earnings, reasonable expectations and great management.

BECOME A SEMESTER INVESTOR

"Buy and Hold" doesn't work as its being promulgated by the so-called bigwigs. It is an ineffective way to build wealth. Even real estate eventually peaks. You could buy an apartment complex, live off of it, take care of it, and watch it grow. At some point, though, with your basis low, and more "deferred maintenance" needing done than you have the inclination for, it might be time to move on. Let new money fix it up.

To everything there is a season. A time to buy, a time to sell. A time to dump losers, a time to capture profits. This time is a season, like a semester in school—a beginning, mid terms, and an end.

I propose that you look at investments with a new "term" outlook. Become a Semester Investor. Think in terms of months, rather than years or decades. Pay more attention to your holdings. Make your money work harder and be prepared—totally unemotionally—to move on.

A SEMESTER INVESTOR does the following:

a) Knows what is wanted from each investment.
b) Position trades: gets money in the way of movements—both up and down.
c) Uses leverage (options) to advantage.
d) Learns and uses selling positions—for instance, calls and puts—to generate income.
e) Weeds the garden better, unloading stocks past their usefulness.
f) Learns cash flow formulas to a "T." Precision produces profits.
g) Avoids fads—sticks with fundamentals like earnings, low debt, revenue increases.

h) Diversifies into formulas.
i) Does not "dollar cost average" down. He/she waits for support levels, and then trades on timely upswings.
j) Knows the quarterly "news-go-round" and measures not only the quantity but the *quality* of news. (See the *Red Light, Green Light* Home Study Course by Wade Cook)
k) Questions everything. The "why is more important than the "how."

"The person who knows how will always have a job.
The person who knows why will always be his own boss."
~Diane Ravitch

l) Keeps increasing his/her skill level. Education is a way of life.
m) Is self correcting—always improving.

Discipline yourself, and others won't have to.
~John Wooden

n) Surrounds himself or herself with like-minded winners.

Now let's address the issue of owning a losing stock. You really have *seven choices:*

1. Continue to hold the stock.
2. Sell the bugger. Use your money elsewhere.
3. If you really like the stock, buy more.
4. Write covered calls against the stock to bring in more cash.
5. Do a LOCC—covered calls with a twist.
6. Rolling Covered Calls
7. Buy One—Sell Two (See on www.wadecook.org for more information)

"Success comes from you, not to you."
~ Wade B. Cook

CHAPTER SIX
HOW MUCH DOES IT TAKE TO GET STARTED? Hint: $1,200

Do you really know where you want to end up? Are you buying into my $8,000 a month? Do you need twice that, or half that amount? I can give you a blueprint, directions and enough details to make the trip possible. But to make a trip, using a map, you must at least know where you are.

If you need to allocate or reallocate assets, that's up to you. See the last chapter for more on this. The point I'm trying to make is that you need some money to get started. It could be as little as $1,200, but truly you'll need $5,000 to $10,000 to do justice. You see, if you don't have a sufficient amount to get started, the commissions (expenses of sales) will eat up the profits.

Suppose we start with $1,200. This amount will buy 1000 shares of a $2.40 stock. That's $2,400, but margin (if the brokerage firm will allow margin investing with this small of an amount) will use up your $1,200. You would only do this if the stock has options and also if the $2.50 strike price on options is available. If the $2.50 calls are going for a quarter, you would take in $250. Commissions would be a total of $80 that is $50 for the stock purchase and $30 for selling the options. Your net would be $170. You'd also make another $100 if the stock is sold for $2,500. You'd also have one more commission. Take $30 out of the $100. You would have a $250 profit. That's not much, but it's fairly certain (at least $170 is certain). $250 on a $1,200 investment is pretty good. This can be done fairly easily.

You may want to buy a $5.00 stock, but only buy 500 shares. Then write the $5 calls. Then use some of the rest of the buy back strategies to make more.

For you skeptics, this small amount may be good for you. You are able to learn skills, build confidence and make money simultaneously. You prove the formula to yourself.

MOVE UP

A tax refund, a gift, a small loan can move you up to $5,000 to $10,000 in working capital. You've seen examples in this book and you'll see dozens of examples and possibilities on T.S.T ™ (Thousand Dollar Thursday) at www.wadecook.org.Ten thousand dollars will buy $20,000 worth of stock. Put in your stop-losses. Shop around. Check out option prices and when you're satisfied, place the order. You'll soon see that $20,000 (or close to it) in stock value will produce $1,500 to $2,000. That's 8% to 10% per month on your $20,000, but is 15% to 20% on your original cash. These results can be increased if you use the buy back and sell the calls more than once per month.

Don't think you can do it? Here are some possibilities for your consideration. At this time there are only four weeks left to July expiration, so we have one month until expiration.

I checked out several stocks. Following in the "not now" category were QLTI, UNTD, XING, CHU, JNPR, MU, AMTD, THOR, and PTEN. This is a lot of shopping to find three deals. I decided on GRA, ELN, and STSI.

Table 1

# Shares	Ticker	Stock Price	1/2 Margin	Strike Option Price	Premium	Called Out/ Not	Net Profit
1,000	GRA	$9.65	$4,825	$10@.50	$500	$350	$850
1,000	ELN	$7.11	$3,555	$7.50@.50	$500	$390	$890
1,000	STSI	$4.88	$2,440	$5@.60	$600	$120	$720
TOTALS			$10,820				$2,460

Our net profit of $2,460 is not quite 23% on our cash, but remember this is just for four weeks. Also, with margin the call premium is based on about $20,000, or two times $10,000. That represents about an 11% return for one month.

Of note also, bear in mind we are not adjusting the rate of return for the option premium cash we have taken in. In reality your broker's computer just recognizes the $2,460 ($850 + $890 + $720) as money in the account. This money will first apply to any margin. Okay, so if that's the case, you have more buying power. Anyway, if we need this $2,460 to adjust our own cash invested of $10,820, we'd be in the $8,400 range with our own cash and the 10% return is realistic.

The time involved to accomplish these trades was about thirty minutes. That's right. Looking at all the stocks that would and would not work. And then, as I was getting ready to take my wife out and run a few errands, I had to wait for her to get ready. Yes, that's unusual, ha!ha! Not one to waste too much time, I looked into a few more companies. They were: AAII, SNDK, MTLG, SEBL, RHAT, CRUS, OCA, PKS, and CHINA.

Again, most of these didn't work. At least not now. But let's take another $10,000, and buy another $20,000 worth of stock and see if we can make another $1,000 profit.

Table 2

# Shares	Ticker	Stock Price	1/2 Margin	Strike Option Price	Premium	Called Out/ Not	Net Profit
500	IIJI	$11.30	$2,825	$12.50@$1.10	$550	$600	$1,150
1000	LEXR	$5.94	$2,970	$7.50@.35	$350	$1,560	$1,910
1000	TIVO	$6.96	$3,480	AUG$7.50@.50	$500	$540	$1,040
TOTALS			$9,275		$1,400		$4,100

We're looking at the August options on TIVO. But look at the combined return! We take in $1,400 on $9,275. Yes, the TIVO is tied up until August but think about two more things:

1. We are doing these trades simultaneously. Usually, we buy on dips, wait and sell on strength. Even if we picked up another ten cents on each trade that would add $300 on to both of these groups of trades. In table #1, we would now make $2,760, and in table #2, we'd make $4,400 instead of $4,100.

2. We're only doing one trade on each of these stocks. What if we can buy back the option, and sell it again on even one or two of these? Our profits would soar. To me, the extra profits will balance out not getting called out. And, if you don't get called out, you still have the stock to sell calls again.

Let's look at one more trade on IMMR. The stock is at $7.10, the $7.50 calls are 50 cents. That's $500 in plus $400 more if we get called out. $3550 to make $500 or $900. Do you see how fun this is?

I have to finish this section with a question and a thought for added growth. Do you need to pull out the cash? Even with $1,200 to $5,000 making $250 to $1,000 this month, if you don't need to pull it out of your account, think what you could build up. Also, this is how it will be in your IRA. You leave the money in and it keeps compounding.

Sometimes you have to wait for the second month's income to buy the next grouping of stocks. Also, as the stocks climb in value, you can keep buying back the options and move up to the higher strike prices. I bought Qualcom at $23 and $26. I wrote the $30 calls, and the $32.50, and the $40 calls. I finally got called out at $42.50. One month, from expiration to expiration I sold and bought back the option five times.

So, yes, you can start with smaller sums. You just need to (a) select better stocks, (b) guard the money better, and (c) work a little harder.

Do you think this can be done with $1,200? Look at the following trade: XOMA was $2.60. 1000 shares would cost $2,600, or $1,300 on margin. Okay, so it's not $1,200, but remember we were trying to make 10%--which would be $120 on $1,200 or $260 on $2,600. The

February $2.50 calls were 50 cents. Sell and take in $500. Now, you'll lose $100 on the stock sale if it stays above $2.50 and if you do not buy it back. The profit of $400 for seven weeks can be used to pay the bills if you want. That's a 30% plus return.

How about this one? ChinaDotcom (Ticker CHINA) was $4.60. Let's buy 500 shares for $2,300 or $1,150 on margin. Sell the $5 calls for January (3 weeks) for 35 cents. You take in $175, which is way over 10% on the investment, but wait, there's more. If the stock moves up and over $5.00, which it looks like it wants to do, you'll make an extra $200 (buy stock for $2300, sell it for $2500). Now the profit would be $375 on the $1,150 cash put up. Not bad at all!

CAN I GET CALLED OUT EARLY?

When you write a covered call you are giving someone the right to buy your stock at a certain price on or before the expiration date. To get called out early, someone would have to actually exercise their option to buy the stock. Computers would whirl away and you might randomly be selected and your stock will be sold—all or part of it.

This rarely happens. In fact it happens so infrequently, I dub this a seminar question. In real life I've had thousands of trades and I've only been called out early a few times.

I'll never forget the time in Sacramento I was teaching a covered call seminar when a gentleman in the front row, looking and sounding very angry, shouted out, "But what if you get called out early?" It was a challenge. Whenever I find myself in such a position, I turn to the audience. "How about it?" I ask them. "How many of you would like to get called out early?" Almost every hand in the audience went up.

By selling early (before the expiration date) you are rushing all of your profits to the "now". The trade is over. You keep the option premium(s) and the profit from selling the stock. The cash is in your account and you're free to move on.

So why doesn't it happen very often?

1. Most investors who trade options are not doing so to actually exercise on the option and actually buy the stock. They buy options, wait for a movement (up or down) and sell—at a profit or loss. In fact, I've never exercised an option and purchased the stock.

2. In order to get called out early the stock would have to be in-the-money. This means the stock price is above the strike price. Example: You bought a stock at $7.20. You then sold the $7.50 calls for 60 cents. The stock rises to $11.50 and its holding firm. If you do nothing, then you will get called out at $7.50. You keep the 60 cents ($600, $6000—whatever) and you make an additional 30 cents on the stock times however many shares you owned.

Will you definitely get called out? Yes, at expiration, but not necessarily before. Why not? Because there has to be someone actually exercising their option to buy the stock. Also, you would very rarely get called out early if there is any time value in the option premium.

This is a little difficult to understand the first time through it. But learn it well because you'll need this knowledge for decision making on whether to buy back the option early. In our example the stock is at $11.50. That's $4.00 above the strike. The $7.50 calls are $4.10 x $4.20. Not much time value as $4 of this price is in-the-money (intrinsic value). Twenty cents is time value.

It would cost $4.20 or $4,200 to buy back the call and end the obligation. We would only do this if we can better our position—say, sell the $10 calls out another month or two.

Why do you not often get called out early? Follow the money. Option market makers are the kind of people who try to make a tenth of a penny on a million transactions a day. To them 10 cents to 20 cents is huge. Even 5 cents is huge. If someone were to exercise on the $7.50 strike price option they would have to lose the 10 cents or 20 cents. They won't do it. If the stock were to stay the same, and get close to expiration, and the option goes to $3.90 x $4.00, you might get called out early. You see there is now no time value. If there is any time value in the premium, it's really unlikely that you'll get called out early.

DECISIONS

If you have a stock that is in-the-money, you can monitor it more closely. If you don't mind getting called out, you can just go about your business. But, if you want to keep the stock for more covered call writing, then you can watch, set alerts, or even set a hard order to buy back the call.

You're in control. And even if you get called out early, in spite of your best efforts, you were profitable. Time to celebrate.

"I don't buy options to actually buy the stock,
and I don't write covered calls to actually sell the stock."
~Wade Cook

A UNIQUE TWIST

Getting called out early hardly ever happens, but remember how excited to get called out early the people in Sacramento were. They wanted to have the trade ended early. With this in mind let me give you another out. If the market won't end the trade early, how about we do it ourselves?

Here's the scenario. I bought TIVO at $4.90 and sold the $5 calls for 55cents. I took in $550. If I get called out at $5 I'll make another 10 cents per share, or $100. Unless I buy it back and resell the call, that $650 is all I'm going to make.

The stock has gone up to $6.30, and it doesn't look like its going to back off. There are still three weeks to expiration. Today the $5 calls were going for $1.35 x $1.40. I could spend $1,400 and recapture the upside of the stock. Then I could sell out another month, or wait and sell a call later.

The stock is midway between two strike prices. The $7.50's aren't going for much. What if I have a better place to use the money? Here's my point: consider buying back the call and then just sell the stock now. Spend the $1,400 to buy the call and sell the stock for $6.30, or $6,300.

Let's review. Stock purchase at $4,900 ($2,450 on margin), sell at $6,300. Profit is $1,400. We sold the call for $500 (remember this number) and spent $1,400 to buy it back. Our net on the call sale and repurchase is minus $900. Subtract the $900 from $1,400 and we have our profit of $500. Yes there are extra commissions, but you had a few anyway. So we make $380 or $400. Remember our original cash in was $2,450. Anyway you cut it, its over 10% for a week or so.

Okay, I could make another hundred dollars or so if I let it go to expiration, but that's three weeks away. What if there is another deal right now, where I can use the same $2,450 and make another $400 to $500? It's about employing your money properly and more efficiently.

The original TIVO trade is over. You have all of your cash back so you can get on to the next trade. I know I've gone through this quickly, and that's because you won't do this very often. But it's another strategy to use—another tool in your tool chest.

WHAT CAN I DO WITH THE MONEY ONCE THE TRADE IS OVER?

1. Spend your profits. I don't think you need help in this department.
2. Add to your asset base. One of the greatest side benefits of writing covered calls is that you start to figure out a stock's movements and patterns. You notice the newsy periods, how the stock is affected. You start to connect the dots better. If you like this stock, maybe buy more.
3. Buy stock in another company.
4. Sell calls again—at a higher strike price. Move up. Sell calls out further.
5. Sell the stock and move your money into a better stock. Remember, there are certain types of stock movements and levels of option premiums that make certain stocks able to produce more certain cash flow. Keep asking, "What else could I be doing with my money?"
6. Wait. You've received cash, now maybe you should wait for the stock to move. Note: see more on the "buy back" later.

PROTECTING THE DOWNSIDE

There are four things you can do to protect the downside movement of the stock.

1. Do better homework. Only buy stocks after paper trading. Make sure the companies are healthy—increasing their earnings growth. Check out premiums, see if they're large enough to make it worthwhile. In short, buy quality.
2. Put in stop-loss orders. You can place an order to sell the stock if it tanks. You need to be comfortable here. If you buy a stock at $8, set the stop loss at $7 or $6.50. What are you willing to lose? You can write the $10 calls just as easily as $7.50. If you're in it for the cash flow you may want to do what I do. I place stop losses slightly under hard support. Ask your broker for the 40 or 50 day moving average. Look at this example on TIVO.

3. If you have a very volatile stock and it has climbed up rapidly, sell the in-the-money call. Pick up more cash now, and as it backs off use the buy back and roll-out.
4. Buy a put. A put option goes up in value as the stock goes down. Sometimes these are called protective puts. Let's say you buy an $18 put and it moves to $19.20. The $20 calls are $1.10. You have 500 shares and take in $550. The $17.50 puts are 10 cents

to buy. You spend 10 cents, $50 (5 contracts) as an insurance policy. If the stock tanks, the $17.50 put could be worth 50 cents to $1.00. You can also buy the $17.50 put and enter a stop loss at $18.00. These are two unrelated transactions, but with s simple purpose—to protect the downside.

Summary:
If you do #1 RIGHT—and choose quality stocks—you'll rarely need #2 and #4. You'll sell in-the-money calls (#3) all the time.

QUESTION: HOW DO I CHOOSE A GOOD BROKER?

A stock broker can really help. We need to choose a technician type broker. These questions and suggestions will help.

I believe that our stockbroker should be a really good tactician, very proficient at keeping us out of trouble and helping us see things we don't see. When you read the first paragraph or two about trade suitability below, you will see my analogy of what a coach does. From this, determine what it is you want your stockbroker to do.

The brokerage firm calls this "trade suitability." This means determining if the type of trade is right for you. As you grow in expertise and competence in any particular strategy and especially as your account starts to grow, you will be able to add to your repertoire of available strategies. But, at the beginning, what you will be able to do in your account might have some severe restrictions. To me this is acceptable.

Hopefully your coaches/brokers in the stock market will do several of the following:

1) Will they bring deals to the table? Do they know what you are looking for and spend time finding stocks and options that fit the types of trades you hope to do?

2) Do they keep abreast of what is going on in the marketplace? Are they good at connecting-the-dots and seeing announcements and pre-announcements as well as becoming efficient at the anticipation of news announcements?
3) Do they like, indeed might I say love, being a stockbroker, and the mechanics of conducting good trades?
4) Have they paid for extra software programs or computer systems to make sure they are getting trades, not only in a timely manner, but also at good fill prices? These software programs can cost way over $1,000 a month. Most large brokerage firms will not pay for their new stockbrokers to have access to this level of trading. They may think they are really good, but they do not have experience with the high tech gadgetry that is available in this business. If you have a new retail stockbroker, they may be very limited on what they can do.
5) Do they love teaching? I know this sounds strange, but we all need to continually be in the educational mode. The target for making profits in the stock market is always shifting. A wise person realizes this but also surrounds himself with people who have the same realization and hopefully people who are very good at explaining things. That is my point: some people might know something but do not know how to convey knowledge about it. Other people are very good at bringing their customers up to speed and educating them in such a manner that everyone is on the same page.
6) Will they avoid unauthorized trades? You can give them authorization, and might I add in writing, to conduct certain trades up to a certain dollar amount. You could also do those trades yourself by putting buy orders and sell orders when you cannot be accessible.
7) Do they have a great reverence for the stock market? Have they been through good times and bad times and know that sometimes making profits in the stock market is just as much an art as it is a science?

John Wooden, the former coach of the UCLA basketball team, and also known as the Wizard of Westwood said a very important thing to his players. Now remember these players are young college basketball stars. In their own mind they are the cat's meow. I cannot imagine any one of his players, traveling across the country to a far away city, 8:30 at night, the time they should go to bed because they have practice the next morning, actually wanting to go to bed. They want to go out and party. John Wooden said to these young players, "Discipline yourselves and others won't have to." What a powerful statement. I suggest that statement to all of us. Again, as a new investor most do not have the required discipline and therefore need a live, passionate, courteous and knowledge-able stockbroker helping to decide which trades are best, when and why, and then implementing the how-to's in an effective manner.

CHAPTER SEVEN
WHAT IS THE BUY-BACK?

Let's get right to it with the amazing "Buy-Back". I've hinted at it all over this book. Once again some of these points will be in the problem-solution format.

The Buy-Back is a simple way of ending a position. If you could hear your stockbroker place the order, it would go something like this. "I (we) want to sell 10 contracts of the Jan. $7.50 calls on Elan (ELN), to open." To open means you've opened up a position on your stock. This time it's a covered call. You own the stock, which you bought at $7.00. Open in this case means you've taken on an obligation to sell the stock at $7.50 anytime on or before the expiration date.

By writing a covered call you have generated income now, but you've sold away everything above the strike price, in this case $7.50. If the position is still open, you can end the covered call obligation. Example: the stock moves to $7.40 and could go above $7.50. It's Wednesday of expiration week and you don't want to sell the stock. You sold the call for $.60, taking in $600 two weeks ago, and even though the stock has moved up, the time is almost gone. The current price on the $7.50 call is 15 cents. It would cost you $150 to buy back the option. Your broker, either online or on the phone, will say something like this to his option desk: "I want to buy 10 contracts, all or none, of the Jan. $7.50 calls at a limit of 15 cents to close the position."

To do a pure buy back you do exactly the opposite of your original trade to get out (close) and mirror what you did to get in (open). You may never use the term "buy-back." It's my term. However, everyone knows it now. You sold to open, you bought to close. To your broker's computer it is a wash. In short, there is no "sold" or "short" position on the stock. Your stock is free and clear. You're ready to rock and roll again.

Now, you sell the $7.50 call for February. They're priced at 80 cents and you take into your account another $800. Your original premium of $600 became $450 after spending $150 to end the covered call position for January. Now add to $450 the February premium of $800 and your total is $1,250. By the way, if you used margin on $7,000, or $3,500 you've recovered one-third of your cash. With the extra $1.25 per share ($1,250 / 1000 shares), this stock would have to drop from $7.00 to $5.75 for you to lose money.

If we did not buy back the $7.50 calls on the Wednesday before Friday expiration, we would probably still own the stock, unless it went above and stayed above $7.50 on Friday. Let's look at this more closely. If we get called out, we will have sold the stock for $7,500 and make $500 capital gain plus the $600 option premium we sold. That's $1,100. But by using the buy-back strategy, our profit is $1,250 cash in without selling the stock. We have the built in capital gain, but unrecognizable for tax purposes because we haven't sold the stock. We also have the stock to write March, April and May covered calls.

If we don't sell the stock on expiration, we keep the $150 we would have spent to buy back the position, and on Monday or later, we can write another covered call. The stock could be up or down compared to Friday. So we sell now or wait and sell the call later.

MOVING ON

Let's do the buy back for $150 for this example. Let's also sell the February call for $800. The stock moves up but on Thursday, just five days later, the stock dips 70 cents. It's going for $6.90 and the February $7.50 calls are .20 x .25. We place an order to buy them back at 20 cents and in a few hours when the stock goes down another 10 cents we are confirmed at 20 cents. This buyback costs us $200. The stock even dropped a bit more—we could have purchased the calls for 15 cents, but we're happy anyway.

It takes two weeks for the stock to work its way back up to $7.50. When it does, we are heading into the second week of February. The $7.50 calls are 45 cents. We sell, taking in $450. I'm going to put here the sells and buy backs I actually did on Star Scientific. Over four months, I took in $6,750 on about $5,285 as the foundation. (See chart on page 4)

The buy back is really not that difficult to do. Everything can be done with standing orders. You sell for 80 cents and put in an order to buy back at 25 cents. Why 25 cents; because you would be happy with a 55 cent profit. You can talk it over with your broker. "What would the stock price have to get down to for the $7.50 calls to go for a quarter?" She says, "Probably $7.20, but you know if it hits $7.00 or even $6.90 they might go for 15 cents." You tell her to set a hard order at 15 cents to buy back the call, but you also ask her to set an alert at 25 cents. If the option trade is there you want her to look hard at it and either call you, or sell it right then, or wait for it to dip a little more. Once you buy it back, you can immediately place an order to sell it again. Would you be happy to sell the $7.50 call for 50 cents again? That would put another $500 in your account—another car payment. Are we having fun yet?

Here's a weird scenario. The $7.00 stock moves up to $11. You've written the $7.50 call. You will most likely get called out. Should you buy back the $7.50 calls? They're going for $3.70. That would cost $3,700! You can write the $10 calls for $1.80, or $1,800. Tough choices. What would you accomplish? You took in $800 the first time. You would spend $3,700 to end the position. You're underwater by $2,900, but then you take in $1,800. You're now only down $1,100. Sounds bad—or does it? You've moved up $2.50 on the strike price. If you're called out at $10 you make $3,000 ($7,000 purchase price to $10,000). You're now up $1,900.

If you left the position in place, you would have made $800 on the call premium plus $500 for gains selling the stock, or $1,300. Some of the decision making process comes down to "do you have the money"-- $3,700? Is this the best use of your money?

One thing you've done is stay in the game. The stock has moved up nicely and very quickly. You could:

1. Wait for the $11 stock to back off and make the buy back decision in a week or two.
2. Do the buy back and roll-up and wait for the stock to back off and buy back the $10 call at that time, or one of my favorites,
3. What if you could sell the next month out option (say March) for $2.80? You'd take in $2,800. Now you're about to break even and you're still in the game. It depends on the answer to the question—Do you want to sell?

By being in the game you have the position tied up longer, so you place orders to buy back and resell the March calls. See how many times you can do this? From my experience, if a stock runs up this quickly, the new high price can't be sustained. Look at these charts:

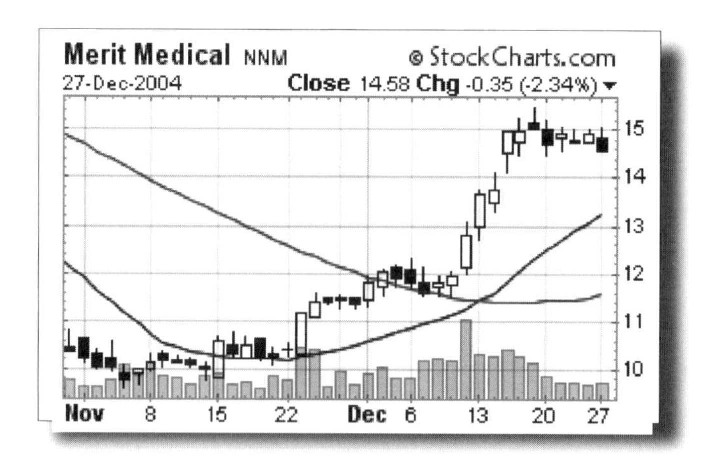

I sold the $12.50 calls, it ran to $15 plus, then backed off.

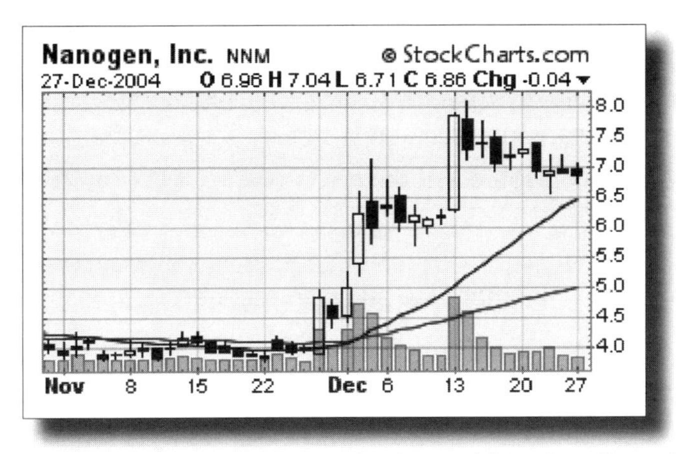

I've played this several times at the $5 and $7.50 strike prices.

I'm going on my third trade and, I've only
had the stock for a month. See www.wadecook.org for more.

Double-dipping is the name of the game. Some of you, who have more passion for this, will even see three and four trades per month on some stocks.

BETTER YOUR POSITION

Now that we've gone through this example, let me paint the big picture and then more specific details.

WE ONLY USE THE BUY BACK TO BETTER OUR POSITION. We don't use the buy back just because we can. We use it to keep the stock, prepare for the next up-tick, and keep the stock working for us multiple times. Remember the all important question: "Do I want to sell the stock, or not?" Upon this question will all of your decisions be based. The buy back allows you to stay in control of the upside movement of the stock and capture two, three and four premiums in one month. Without it, you're left with one monthly premium and you're left at the whim of the market—Is the stock above or below the strike price? You don't want to be out of control.

BIGGER, BETTER, QUICKER

1. The buy back with standing orders and alerts allows you to monitor the stock movements. You only need a few stocks that move 50 cents to $1.50 in repeated patterns to really bump up your income.
2. When you buy back the call, you free up all of your choices:
   - Do nothing, wait
   - Sell the stock—all or part
   - Buy more stock, at good support levels
   - Write calls at different strike prices—move up or down
   - Write calls, now or in a short time, for larger premiums—say out 5 to 7 months. See "LOCC" in Reference Materials
   - You've ended this trade. The profits are certain. You sold for $800 and bought back for $150. Your $650 is in the account. This trade is off your plate.
   - You own the stock, you're in control. You ask the "Do I want to sell?" question again and again to help you make valuable decisions.

In short, the buy back is a way of helping you make "correctable decisions" not just correct decisions.

CHAPTER EIGHT
REAL DEALS, REAL PROFITS

The following is a miscellaneous selection of emails which we send out every Thursday. We call this TDT or Thousand Dollar Thursday. We show many trades, where with $4,000 to $5,000 you can net around $1,000. Our theme: "A Grand New Deal Every Week." Just imagine receiving this at your home or office every week. What I'm hoping you ask is: "How have I been able to live without these?"

THE MINEFIELD

Trading and Investing in the stock market is fraught with danger. Imagine this…You've got to get your troops across a mine field. Scenario One: Standing by the field is a man telling you that for $100 he'll point out the way for you to go. Using his advice you should miss the danger spots. Scenario Two: Another man says that for $400 he'll sell you a map. It has a path, with the mines detailed, and you should be successful getting across. Scenario Three: The next man says that for $1,000 he'll take you through the field. He'll take your hand and lead you. He's been through many times. You can step where he steps, guaranteeing your successful completion.

Point: Wade Cook will take you through the minefield.

ENJOY: There's a lot to learn here, besides just the numbers on potential trades.

Wade Cook's TDT

THOUSAND DOLLAR THURSDAY

June 16, 2005

Would it surprise you...

- ...if the most effective way to build up cash flowing assets is a simple "one-two" formula?
- ...if there was a way to get million-dollar income from $8,500?
- ...if one to four hours a month made you more money than working 40 hours a week—four weeks a month?

If we're looking for a more active way of trading on good investments, covered call writing provides the ability to notch it up. First of all, a simple position trade. Many of you own stocks. What most of you do not know is that you can make extra income, actual spendable cash income, by selling an option against your position. Let's move away from the stock market and use real estate to elucidate this matter.

You own a $300,000 property. Someone will give you $5,000 (option money) and purchase the right to buy your property at $320,000. The purchase time is say three months. Now what will happen? They will either come through with the purchase or not. Either way you keep the $5,000. If they don't come through and exercise their option, you still own the property. You can sell it outright, keep it, sell another option at $300,000, $320,000 or even $350,000.

If you were willing to sell it for $300,000 (within 3 months), would you want more money? I would—at least $10,000 now, maybe $15,000.

I've just described "writing covered calls." Write means to sell; covered means you actually own the stock. A call is the option. Many people buy options, hoping the stock will go up. That's very risky. Back to our real estate example: If the purchaser didn't actually want to buy the property, but wanted to sell his $5,000 option for $7,000 or $10,000, what would have to happen? The property would have to be a bargain, or grow in value, or a ready buyer would have to be in the wings. Which of these scenarios do you control? Now, as the seller, we have the $5,000. Property goes up or down—what do we care? Time marches on—its our friend, not our enemy.

Back to our stock position. Options are in 100 share contracts. Strike prices are set in $2.50 or $5.00 increments on most stocks. Some have $1.00 increments (AMD, MU,).

Examples: (Find in here your own "GRAND NEW DEAL EVERY WEEK.") We'll do 1,000 shares of each of these, except STSI (2,000).

<table>
<tr><th>TICKER</th><th>PRICE</th><th>÷2
MARGIN</th><th>OPTION$</th><th>MONTH
STRIKE</th><th>PROFIT
If called out</th></tr>
<tr><td>ELN</td><td>$7.20</td><td>$3,600</td><td>$.50</td><td>July
$7.50C</td><td>$800</td></tr>
<tr><td colspan="6">Take in $500 on the option and an extra $300 if called out.</td></tr>
<tr><td>IIJI</td><td>$10.70</td><td>$5,350</td><td>$1.75</td><td>July
$10.00C</td><td>$ 1,050</td></tr>
<tr><td colspan="6">Take in $1,750, but you lose $700 if called out writing the $10C</td></tr>
<tr><td>IIJI</td><td>$ 10.70</td><td>$5,350</td><td>$.80</td><td>July
$12.50C</td><td>$2,600</td></tr>
<tr><td colspan="6">Same stock as above. Questionable if stock will go above $12.50, but
If it does you'd make $1,800 more and make $2,600 (+the $800 option).</td></tr>
<tr><td>STSI</td><td>$4.80</td><td>$4,800</td><td>$.55</td><td>July
$5C</td><td>$1,500</td></tr>
<tr><td colspan="6">2000 share (20 contract) basis.
Take in $1,100 on the option plus $400 if called out.</td></tr>
</table>

<table>
<tr><td>GRA</td><td>$9.90</td><td>$4,950</td><td>$.60</td><td>July
$10.00C</td><td>$700</td></tr>
<tr><td colspan="6">Take in $600 on the option plus $100 if called out (sold)</td></tr>
<tr><td>IDCC</td><td>$17.86</td><td>$8,930</td><td>$ 1.45</td><td>July
$17.50C</td><td>$890</td></tr>
<tr><td colspan="6">Take in $1,450 on the option, but give back $360 if sold</td></tr>
<tr><td>IDCC</td><td>$17.86</td><td>$8,930</td><td>$.55</td><td>July
$20.00C</td><td>$2,690</td></tr>
<tr><td colspan="6">Same stock as above. Take in $550 now, plus $2,140 if called out at $20.00. Added together, this trade COULD net you $2,690</td></tr>
</table>

Note: Just like our real estate, you get paid more cash now to sell at a lower price. On the higher sell price, you take in less now, but potentially more later.

Note2: I (Wade Cook) am in all of these stocks.

Is this fun or what? You can be more active and make more money if you choose. For example, on IDCC, I sold the $20 calls last week, bought them back—netted $400. Now, I've taken in $700 more. On STSI, my $5,285 has netted $6,750 in 3 months. That's about $2,000 a month on the $5,285.

Look at the second question—getting a million dollar income from $8,500. $1,000,000 in the bank at 3% produces $30,000 a year. Look at a few of these trades. $8,930 (IDCC) makes $2,690 this month x 12 = $32,280. $10,700 (IIJI) makes $31,200. You won't do this month's numbers every month, but two points (1) There are good deals like these every month; (2) This is only one trade—if we employ the buy-back and double dip we can make way more—like STSI. $5,285 is on track to make over $20,000 this year. Yes, we walk the walk.

This is just not that tough to do. You don't need a lot of time—maybe 2 to 5 hours a month (to manage 12 to 20 positions); you don't need to know everything about the market. We're here to help with training (TNT), constant access to our trades (TST), a trade every day on our site (PT3) and these Thursday emails (TDT). We'd love to help you take $10,000 and show you how to produce $3,000 to $4,000 a month with it. Quit your job someday. Live a better life.

It's funny when people ask what all of our services cost. There's a world of difference between price and cost. The price is $44 for TNT and we're currently including for free TST, TDT, and DT3. The cost? If you take $1,000 and make $300, what is the cost? It could cost you $100,000 a year to not participate. We're here to help you retire (within six months) cash flow wealthy.

"Wade Cook doesn't break the rules, he rewrites them."

See your LNI Affiliate or call toll free 1-866-579-5900 to subscribe.

Note: We have an Affiliate Program available. You can make 25% plus with our program. Call the same number above.

Wade Cook's TDT
THOUSAND DOLLAR THURSDAY
June 9, 2005

PISTONS vs. SPURS. I wish both teams well and hope they stay healthy for a great series. What a great country we live in! There are opportunities everywhere. Here is a deal I did yesterday. A reminder—we attempt to take $4,000 to $5,000 and have it make a GRAND--$1,000, over the next month. Our really big profits come from "multiple hits," or in other words—getting our assets to produce income several times a month; sort of like "rental stock" with the rent due two to three times a month. Read on to the C and E sections.

A. Interdigital Communications (IDCC). Stock was $18.45. I bought 500 shares for $9,225, but about $4,600 on margin. I then sold the July $20 calls (rental stock income) for $1.55. 500 shares allow me to sell 5 contracts and take in $775. So you say, "Hey, Wade—that's not $1,000!" Yes but if the stock moves up and I get called out (sell my stock) at $20, I'll make another $1.55 times 500 shares, or $775. That will add up to $1,550—yes on my $4,600. And, this original $775 for selling the call is just one time. Doing covered calls the Wade Cook way becomes your very own retirement system!

B. For years I've tried to get peoples attention, have them stop and really think about a way to retire "cash flow wealthy"—NOW. What does it take to get your attention? Testimonials? I've got drawers full. Real Deals? I'm doing about 13 a month now. Education? Check out our TNT, TST and these TDT's.

   Honestly, I don't know how to reach some people. Maybe a question will help. If $4,600 makes $1,650 this month – how many $1,650's do you need to retire? Three would be about $5,000 (cash, this month). Pay the bills. Pay off your mortgage.

Grow out of your problems. Look again. $15,000 (assets) lets the average family retire. Oops! There I go. I know, you're not average. But, what if . . .?

Now, my attempt is to move the assets down to $10,000 and by working a little harder (double-dipping) have it still make you $4500 to $5000 a month. I'm doing it. I'm in the trenches. I'll show you how. Okay, so, what about this? What if I take $5,200 and have it make about $2,000 a month? Let's move on and I'll show you this tracking log.

C. CASH FLOW TRACKING SYSTEM

Stock (co)		Star Scientific		Ticker	STSI	Total Ca Taken In		
Date		# shares		Cost		On margin		
1/31	B	1000	$4.54	$4,540		Batch 1		
2/3	B	1000	$6.03	$6,0		atch 2		
			Totals	$10,5				
Date	B or S	#Contracts	Month	Strike		Cash in/out	Net	al
4/12	S	20	May	5c	$1.00	$2,000		
4/20	B	20	May	5c	($0.50)	($1,000)	$1,000	$2,850
4/26	S	20	June	5c	$0.90	$1,800		
4/27	B	20	June	5c	($0.50)	($1,000)	$800	$3,650
4/27	S	20	June	5c	$0.90	$1,800		
5/16	B	20	June	5c	($0.45)	($900)	$900	$4,550
5/23	S	20	June	5c	$0.70	$1,400		
6/7	B	20	June	5c	($0.60)	($1,200)	$200	$4,750
6/7	S	20	July	5c	$1.00	$2,000		
						$0	$2,000	$6,750

From 1/3/05 to 4/12/05 Wade has done 6 round trip trades on STSI producing $1,850

$5,285 Invested

$6,750 Cash Flow

$12,035 Current

* This figure represents the amount of cash flow generated from writing covered calls added to the current value of the stock as of the closing price on 6/8/05 of $5.40 and if no money is taken out of the account.

Point: $5,285 has made $6,750. $5,285 in 3 months is now $12,035. I still have the 2,000 shares of STSI and it's poised to double every 2 ½ to 4 months. Do you see your retirement?

D. Here are a few more deals for your consideration. Do your own homework. Note: You'll notice in the last column the phrase "if called out." This means we end up selling the stock at the agreed upon strike price. If a stock is at $14.80 (1000 shares) and we sell it for $15, we make an extra 20¢, or $200. If the stock purchased is $15.20 and we sell it for $15.00 we lose 20¢ or $200. For these examples we add or subtract those amounts to or from the option premium we took in to "net it out." We'll do 1,000 shares of each and sell 10 contracts. There are a few 20% (cash on cash) returns here.

TICKER	PRICE	÷2 MARGIN	OPTION$	MONTH STRIKE	PROFIT If called out
ENCY	$10.00	$5,000	$.60	July $10C	$600
TASR	$10.60	$5,300	$ 1.25	July $10C	$650
LEXR	$ 5.60	$2,800	$.95	July $5C	$350
MYGN	$15.30	$7,650	$.85	July $15C	$550
GRA	$ 9.60	$4,800	$.60	July $10C	$1,000
KFX	$12.75	$6,375	$ 1.20	July $12.50C	$950
STSI	$ 5.30	$2,650	$.95	July $5C	$650

E. Please, don't judge this system by what you know or don't know. Ask yourself: Are these profits worthy of me (or you) spending four to six hours of education time to gain the skills? Henry Ford stated, " If money is your hope for independence you will never have it. The only real security that a man will have in this world is a reserve of knowledge, experience and ability". Then, instead of working 40 to 60 hours a week, how about spending one to two hours a week (or month) making $5,000, $10,000, $20,000 a month? Last question: Does Wade Cook have the skills to train me?

Summary: We just put the ball in your court. Call and subscribe to TNT or stick with the training if you already subscribe.

Wade Cook's

Thousand Dollar Thursday T.D.T.

April 21, 2005

The market sure has been in the doldrums lately. It just doesn't seem to be able to get a foot hold. If you are trading in options, either by buying straight options—calls or puts—or selling options as in spreads, naked puts or in covered call writing, it just means option prices are less expensive. All in all the implied volatility (the VIX) measurement says the market just doesn't want to go anywhere. This basically pulls all the premium out of the options but in covered call writing getting something for selling an option is better than getting nothing.

We have to look harder and longer to find good covered call stocks. Sometimes a covered call stock that has a big premium is almost too risky. However, as I was talking last week I still think W.R. Grace, even this week, still presents great opportunities. It is a couple of dollars higher than last weeks T.D.T. but it is still is an interesting price area. Let's look at a trade and see if we can take $5,000 and make a $1,000 profit.

Here is the trade: Buy 800 shares of W.R. Grace (GRA) at $11.40. That comes to $9,120 Divide by 2 (for margin) = $4.560. We are under $5,000 already. Sell the May $12.50 Calls (which is not even a month away) and take in .95 x 800=$760. If we were to get called out we would make another $1.10 (difference between $12.50 sell price and $11.40 purchase price), or $880. Add it to $760=$1,640. We make the $760, but the only way to make $1,000 is to get called out. If you look at a chart it looks like it is ready to move up.

2nd trade on GRA: Selling in the money calls. We will use the same numbers to buy the stock and then sell the May $10 Calls for $2.20. That would be $1,760 for 800 shares. Subtract $10 from the $11.40

purchase price and we give back $1.40 x 800 shares is $1,120. Now subtract $1,120 (give back) from $1,760 (cash in) = $640 profit.

So once again this could be a good profitable trade. And remember, in covered call writing you don't have to buy 800 shares, you could buy 1800 or 200 shares, but remember to buy shares in 100 lot increments. Option contracts are basically in 100 lots.

Believe it or not STSI still presents some opportunities. The stock is at $4.50 which would be $4,500 divided by 2 (margin) = $2,250. You can still sell the May $5 Calls for .45 which would mean $450 and another $500 if you were to get called out. In this case you get about a 20% return on just writing a covered call and possibly a 40% return if you were to get called out at the $5 strike price.

There have been a lot of questions on the "buy-back" and I am going to continue to cover this process and protecting the downside of the stock in our next T.N.T. (Tuesday Night Training). I hope you can join me and look forward to seeing you there. If you want to try one event for FREE, we will be happy to give you the phone number and a one-time pin to join in on the rollicking excitement.

By the way, look how my attitude changed from the April 21st TDT.

Wade Cook's
THOUSAND DOLLAR THURSDAY
T.D.T.

May 12, 2005

This is the coolest market for writing covered calls that I've seen in a long time. Yes, the market is range bound (stuck!), but there are pretty nice option premiums on many stocks.

For those of you who are stuck—writing covered calls gives you a chance to fight back. By this I mean make actual cash money on your assets. Use this money to pay your bills, add to your account, etc. Simply, it allows you to Grow WealthTM. When most people see the word "option", they back off—and well they should if they buy options. By playing pure options—calls and puts—it's tough to make consistent money. Why? Because the market forces are working against you. The option you buy decreases in value as time deteriorates, etc. The stock had to move big and quickly, or you lose.

Meet NoR.M. No Required Movement. Let's sell (write) an option (call) against a stock we own (covered) and put cash in the account. Now, whether the stock goes up, down or sideways, we make money. A basic truth: stock prices fluctuate. Okay, but for writing a call we've put certain cash in our account—cash we can use!

If you own a stock currently at $10.20 and you write the June $10 calls for $.90, 1000 shares of stock would allow you to take in $900. If you get called out (jargon for sell your stock) you'd have to give back (lose) $.20 per share or $200. You'd net $700. Think about $700 extra cash. What if you bought this stock at $9.20? You'd also have gains of $800 ($10 - $9.20= $.80 or $800).

That's one trade. If you don't want to sell the stock, right up to the expiration you could "buy-back" the obligating call option, end the trade and write the next month out. If the stock is $10.20, the call may cost $2.50, or $250. $900 (-) $250 = $650 net.

Look at these deals! See how many "GRAND" new deals are here. $1000 on $4,000 to $5,000 is just not that tough once you know how.

STOCK (OUT)	TICKER	STOCK PRICE	JUNE STRIKE	OTION (BID)	PROFIT (CALLED OUT)
W.R. Grace $9,700 ÷ 2	GRA = $4,850	$9.70	$10C	$1.35 $1,350	$1,650
Interdigital Comm $15,450 ÷ 2	IDCC = $7,725	$15.45	$15C	$2.20 $2,200	$1,750
Elan $7,700 ÷ 2	ELN = $3,850	$7.70	$7.50C	$1.20 $1,200	$1,000
Nanometrics $10,300 ÷ 2	NANO = $5,150	$10.30	$10C	$ .85 $850	$550
Star Scientific $4,550 ÷ 2	STSI = $2,725	$4.55	$5C	$.50 $500	$950
Taser $11,200 ÷ 2	TASR = $5,600	$11.20	$10C	$1.90 $1,900	$700
Taser $11,200 ÷ 2	TASR = $5,600	$11,20	$12.50C	$.75 $750	$2,050
Nitro $16,400 ÷ 2	NTMD = $8,200	$16.40	$15C	$3.00 $3,000	$1,600
Nitro $16,400 ÷ 2	NTMD = $8,200	$16.40	$17.50C	$1.85 $1,850	$2,950

You figure the rate of return—remember it's 5 ½ weeks until the June Expiration. Pretty awesome! Do you see yourself financially independent?

Wade Cook's
Thousand Dollar Thursday
T.D.T

May 19, 2005

Our TDT today will be about selling an in-the-money call option. Either you are going to write an in the money call or an out of the money call and in this case I want to show you a way of generating more cash into your account.

One of the things that we never discus in relationship to doing a trade on margin, which simply means that we only put up half the money to do the trade, is that when you sell a call option and generate cash into your brokerage account, the brokers computer recognizes that cash as money deposited into the account. That money can be applied towards the margin account. That simply means that you will have less of your own money tied up in the trade. When we are teaching the strategies we rarely use the money that comes into the account to figure a better rate of return. We usually use the full amount on margin to calculate the amount of return we make.

Moving on. When we have a stock that is at $7.70, for example, we would then sell the $7.50 call. You might ask why we are selling a stock for $7.50 that we paid $7.70 and one of the simple reasons is that we generate more cash into the account. Part of an option premium is the amount that is in the money, or what is also called the intrinsic value. In this example .20¢ of the option premium is in-the-money. So that .20¢ represents the part of the stock price that is above the strike price—hence in the money. If the $7.50 June options are selling for .80¢, .20¢ of the .80¢ is the in-the-money portion and the other .60¢ is considered the time value. Obviously when we write covered calls we are looking for stocks with a fair amount of volatility. The time value—or what is also called the implied volatility— is quite large.

This is a classic case of the "The greater the risk, the greater the reward; the lower the risk, the lower the reward." If we find a stock that is fluctuates quite wildly, the option premiums are more than likely going to be more expensive. From a purchasing point of view that means that we have a lot more risk but a chance of making more money. But in writing covered calls we are selling the call and capturing the profits right now. Therefore if we want to make more money we need to find stocks that have a fair amount of volatility to create the extra "fluff" in the option premium.So look at the following examples. Look at each one of these stocks and do your own homework and find out if there has been a lot of fluctuation and movement. You will notice a couple of these where the option premiums are not very pricey and therefore they generate a lot less money into our accounts for writing a covered call. But the safety of those types of stocks also presents an opportunity for those people who like a lot more safety in their investing and trading. Look at NTMD, EYET and AGIX and you will see that the option premiums are really expensive. They are generating returns of 16%, 18%, 20% or more and that is just for one month between now and June. You will see that the rate of profit is really quite substantial and yet the underlying stock is more volatile and could go down as easily as it can go up. But again we are taking in more money and getting a better reward. There is a bit more risk to that. So within this list of stocks and covered call opportunities you should be able to find a few that are compatible with your risk/reward tolerance.

Some examples:

EYET – Stock price was $23.40, the June $22.50 calls were $2.90 x $3.10 or a 17% return.

NTMD – Stock price was $18.56, the June $17.50 calls were $2.95 x $3.10 or a 20% return.

AGIX – Stock price was $15.12, the June $15 calls were $1.20 x $1.35 or a 14% return.

MSFT – Stock price was $25.92, the June $25 calls were $1.10 x $1.15 or a 1% return

INTC – Stock price was $26.01, the June $25 calls were $1.30 x $1.35 or a 2% return.

MOT – Stock price was $17.30, the June $17 calls were .70¢ x .75¢ or a 5%

See you next week. NTMD received an FDA panel approval and the stock went crazy.

4/28/2005
4:35:PM AMD
Wade bought back his May $15 call on AMD today for .25 cents and then put in an order to resell it for .75 cents

4/21/2005
On XXIA I got $1.05 on selling the May $17.50 Calls. It is pretty cool, in a way because, about three weeks ago when I bought the stock, I sold the May $17.50 Calls for $1.45, bought them back a few days later at .35. So I made $1100 on this trade, and I just sold them again today for $1.05, so it is another $1,050 profit.

4/14/2005
I just bought back the April $16 calls on AMD for .70¢ and put in an order to sell the May $17 calls for .95¢, I could sell the May $16 calls for $1.10 and make .15¢ more. Right now the $17 calls are .65¢ x. 75¢ so with a down market I might have to wait until tomorrow or another up tick day to be able to get hit on that.

4/13/2005
He bought 1000 shares of the stock at $8.01 and then sold 10 of the May $7.50 calls at $1.30. He talked about this one on TNT last night.

4/7/2005
He bought 1000 shares of NANO (Nanometrics Inc.) @ $12.54 and then sold 10 of the May $12.50 calls for $1.05. So on this trade he has $6,270 invested to make $1,001 after the give back of .04 cents per share if he is called out.

3/29/2005
Also on RMBS, the stock is down in the low $15 range and I want to increase my ownership to 1000 shares so I put in an order to buy 400 more shares at $15.25. I went ahead and put in an order to sell the May $15 calls at $1.55.

3/25/2005
Another trade that Wade did yesterday was to buy back the 6 contracts of the April $15 calls for $1.30 and then entered an order to sell the May $17.50 calls for $1.45. He has rolled out and moved up a strike price to take advantage of the latest run up in the stock.

3/18/2005
Here is a stock to watch, ONXX- the stock is at $33.00 and the April $35 calls are going for $4.60 x $4.80. The April $30 calls are $7.20 x $7.50.

3/14/2005
On CTIC he was filled on his order to buy back the Apr $5 calls he sold for .25 cents. He has put an order to sell them again at .75 cents. He has now taken in $3,075 cash on one batch and $2,750 on the second batch.

Just think of what results you could achieve if you could look over the shoulder of an experienced trader everyday while he is trading? Many successful people won't even talk to you. Many made their money in such ways that they are not able to be duplicated by the average person. Not Wade. He Shares. He Teaches. He understands many "connect-the-dots" situations and has a passion for teaching. This passion is even stronger than his passion for making money. It's what drives him. He shares so much because he cares so much.

Who else do you know who puts their trades (win, lose or draw) on an Internet site as a tutorial service for the whole world to see? You can see these trades (examples are above) on T.S.T. Trading Skills and Techniques at www.wadecook.org. You may ask, so what? What does this mean to me? Remember, Cash Flow Success comes from the effective application of specific knowledge. Many trades on TST are put forth in a unique way. It's a process—once again, totally to help our students make more money in less time with less risk.

When I taught real estate seminars. I was constantly asked if people could fly in and spend a day or a week with me. They understood the importance of live "experiential" education. It's much easier in the stock market because you can "look over the shoulder" as I make money. My staff also adds much.

This is why we created TST or Trading Skills and Techniques. You can subscribe and then access this information 24/7. These are real trades. Sometimes even longer explanations are given. I've kept it brief here.

CASH FLOW TRACKING SYSTEM

The following is a filled in cash flow tracking system so you can see how it works with real numbers. On the following page you have a blank sheet, feel free to make copies for your own use. Note: You may print out an 8.5 x 11 sheet at www.libertynetwork.us

$8,450 Profit

$5,285 Cash Out

$13,735 Total Value*

Stock (co)		Star Scientific		Ticker	STSI	Total Cash Taken In		
Date		# shares		Cost	On margin			
1/31	B	1000	$4.54	$4,540		Batch 1		
2/3	B	1000	$6.03	$6,030		Batch 2		
			Totals	$10,57				
Date	B or S	#Contracts	Month	Strike		Cash in/out		
1/31	S(1)	10	Feb	5c	$0.60	$600		
2/9	B(1)	10	Feb	5c	($1.30)	($1,300)	($700)	($700)
2/3	S(2)	10	Feb	7.50c	$0.60	$600		
2/9	B(2)	10	Feb	7.50c	($0.30)	($300)	$300	($400)
2/9	S(1)	10	Mar	5c	$1.70	$1,700		
2/24	B(1)	10	Mar	5c	($1.60)	($1,600)	$100	($300)
2/9	S(2)	10	Mar	7.50c	$0.85	$850		
2/23	B(2)	10	Mar	7.50c	($0.40)	($400)	$450	$150
2/25	S	20	Mar	7.50c	$0.45	$900		
3/9	B	20	Mar	7.50c	($0.15)	($300)	$600	$750
3/9	S	20	April	5c	$0.80	$1,600		
4/8	B	20	April	5c	($0.25)	($500)	$1,100	$1,850
4/12	S	20	May	5c	$1.00	$2,000		
4/20	B	20	May	5c	($0.50)	($1,000)	$1,000	$2,850
4/26	S	20	June	5c	$0.90	$1,800		
4/27	B	20	June	5c	($0.50)	($1,000)	$800	$3,650
4/27	S	20	June	5c	$0.90	$1,800		
5/16	B	20	June	5c	($0.45)	($900)	$900	$4,550
5/23	S	20	June	5c	$0.70	$1,400		
6/7	B	20	June	5c	($0.60)	($1,200)	$200	$4,750
6/7	S	20	June	5c	$1.00	$2,000		
6/14	B	20	June	5c	($0.25)	($500)	$1,500	$6,250
6/14	S	20	July	5c	$0.55	$1,100		
6/29	B	20	July	5c	($0.30)	($600)	$500	$6,750
6/29	S	20	Aug	5c	$0.45	$900		
7/20	B	20	Aug	5c	($0.20)	($400)	$500	$7,250
7/22	S	20	Aug	5c	$0.60	$1,200		
						$0	$1,200	$8,450

*This figure represents the amount of cash flow generated from writing covered calls added to the current value of the stock of the close on 7/27/2005 of $4.40

Stock (co)				Ticker		Cash Taken in $		
							Page	
Date	B or S	# shares	Price	Cost	On margin	Notes		
			Totals					

Date	B or S	#Contracts	Month	Strike	Premium	Cash in/out	Net Profit	Accum. Total

CHAPTER NINE
THE EFFECT OF EARNINGS SEASONS REPORTS

Lately, I've spent a lot of time in my seminars talking about and showing people how to increase their powers of observation and apply that to increasing their profits. For example, if you see patterns, say a connection between a company's stock dipping or rising at certain times as the stock goes through a split, can you take advantage of this pattern? Can we make better trades? Can we get in at more opportune times and get out with more cash?

We need to get better at making connections. I look for connections in the stock market all the time and then try to figure out how to capitalize on those observations. I've recently discovered something so pervasive, so recognizable, that once you know and "get it," it will literally shake up a lot of things you do. It will help you avoid mistakes. It will help you trade better—better execution and more cash profits.

What I am about to explain is a price movement phenomenon based on the market's reaction to events on the corporate calendar. Many people have observed parts of this phenomenon. Others see one angle of it but don't see the connection. Still others see the same patterns and time periods but don't understand the "why" behind the stock movements. If you don't truly understand this cause and effect, it's hard to build faith in the process—to formulate your "law" and put that law to work for you.

Your stockbroker or financial planner may claim to have known about this concept. If so, chew that person out for not telling you. Anyway, I doubt they know the entirety of this process. I've not talked to one person yet who understands all of this before I explained it—no broker, surely no news writer or journalist, and no other author.

You are about to read probably the single most important thing about trading in the stock market you have ever read or ever will read. I call it "Red Light – Green Light." This pearl of business wisdom was found through years of struggle, and you minimize this process at your trading peril. Watch and be wise.

CHRONOLOGICAL CONNECTIONS

In May of 1995 I took our company public. Our assets grew rapidly and we became a reporting company June 30, 1996, when the quarterly SEC reports are filed. The June 30 reports actually had to be filed within 45 days, or by August 15. This important point will come back into play later. Read on.

For years my accounting and legal departments have worked on our quarterly and annual reports. During this quarterly process, there are windows which open or close on what I as a CEO, Board member and insider can say. There are also specific time periods when I can and cannot sell my own company's stock.

After years of complying—being careful when to buy and sell, and being careful of what I say and when—I started observing things. Here it is plain and simple: News drives stock prices. Everyone knows this. But what they know is only one component, one piece of the puzzle.

Here's the question I asked myself. If I, as a CEO, am under all these restrictions—these open and closed window periods of time—then what about the 25,000 or so other CEOs, CFOs, COOs, CLOs, Boards of Directors and other insiders of all publicly traded companies in this wonderful country? Are they not under the same requirements?

IMPORTANT DATES

This is where the next piece of the puzzle falls into place. When can "insiders" talk? When do they have to go silent? And what effect does this quarterly phenomenon have on the rise and fall of their stock prices? We'll explain all of these as we move along, but first some important dates.

December 31	This is the year end for most companies SEC filings.
March 31	Annual filings must be submitted, and this document must be audited by an outside firm. The filing deadline is 90 days later, or March 31.
June 30	These are calendar quarter ends. Quarterly SEC
September 30	Filings may be unaudited. Filings are due 45 days later, on May 15, August 15 and November 15. Do you see an overlapping time period in the March 31 area?
December 31	Filings for the previous year need to be made as a company is just finishing up its first quarter.

NEWS—CHANGING PERCEPTIONS

Okay, let's start down the path. It's about June 15—a few weeks before the quarter ends. People start to talk. Analysts adjust and readjust their expected earnings numbers. The CEO of Big Company comes out in interviews or news releases and downplays the numbers, saying something like, "Sales have been good, but we have a charge off, so earnings will be $1.12 instead of $1.32." The stock drops $5, from $86 to $81. Now toward the end of June other news—mergers, share buy-backs, takeovers, stock splits, other sales figures, new product announcements, et cetera, et cetera—hits the streets. The stock wavers but heads back up.

Of all these newsy items, the type of announcement most followed is any announcement having to do with earnings. I've written about earnings, or P/E, in many other places. Many people base what they are willing to pay for a stock on the P/E, or price-to-earnings ratio. A typical NYSE company has a P/E of around 20—let's say 19.2. In short, this means that the stock will cost $19.20 for every $1.00 of earnings. The stock may be at $250 or $5 or 50¢, it matters not. Now a static or isolated P/E is not the only factor in price determination even for those who only follow P/Es. Other important considerations include these questions: Are earnings growing or contracting? How does this company's earnings compare to those of other companies? Are earnings even a viable measurement in certain sectors? Internet stocks are a scary diversion from sound rational practice in stock choices. Many have no "E" in their P/E.

Back to the point: Earnings is the most widely watched measurement of stock values. Because of this, all CEOs must be very careful of what they say about earnings.

Let's move down to the first week of July. The quarter is over, but the actual filing (10Q) has not yet been done. That will happen in a few weeks—at least by August 15, the filing deadline. Now, think this through. If the CEO, CFO or other corporate bigwigs comment about actual numbers before the proper documents are filed, it is assumed that he or she knows what the numbers should be. Do you see? Even if the accountants aren't through with the complete consolidated numbers, it would be determined that he or she should know. Because of this there is a complete news shutdown (shh! no talking, no talking!). No one will talk until the 10Qs are filed and the news release is out. Funny thing—the stock gets back to $86 and even up to $88. How does this happen? There is something happening here. Paranoia strikes deep. It is as if a whole group of people know something we don't know. In fact, we're the last to know.

Here's the pathetic, yet comical irony. Now the news is out—it's official. The interviews or press releases start up with something like this: "Earnings are ahead of expectations by about 10%. They are $1.22 per share." As the report goes on, you'll see an interesting twist. "We're pleased with the numbers and growth, but we contemplate a slowdown in sales next quarter (or year) and may not be able to maintain these high numbers."

Is this crazy or what? They good-mouth and bad-mouth their numbers in the same breath. Why? You must understand the fear these CEOs and others live under. They do not want to be seen hyping their stock. They couch the truth behind caveats. They pad everything. This is the way it is.

Now another unusual thing happens. Many times the stock goes down in spite of good news. It is a strange phenomenon. I'm still perplexed when it happens. It's part of the "buy on rumors, sell on facts (news)" syndrome. Sometimes it has to do with what has happened to the stock in the few weeks or months before the report. It has a lot to do with sentiment—expectations and the like. There are too many variables to mention in this chapter. It's a mystery wrapped in a conundrum engulfed by an enigma.

Do you see how important these topics are? Think of all the guesswork going on by people following the company. Rumor fires are easily kindled. Sometimes they get out of control. However they start, whatever they are, it all ends when the actual numbers and news hit the street.

All of this is very important, but then what? Where's the sequel? Where's the new news? It's now the end of July or first week of August. (The same could be applied to the end of the October/November or January/February or April/May periods.) The news is out. We don't have to wait as long as we did for Episode I—The Phantom Menace—to come out in the Star Wars series, but wait we must. In short, in the absence of news, "this stock ain't going nowhere." The balloon isn't going up without hot air. The car isn't leaving the garage without gas. Superman isn't flying without his cape.

Here's a problem. What if we purchase stock at the height of this incredible (pre) news time? The stock has risen to $92. A big firm puts out a buy rating. Others follow. The company has even announced a stock split for August 20, a Friday. It just looks peachy—how can we lose?

Oh, and what if we like options? Those funny little derivatives which rise and fall as the stock does—and erode as the time moves on toward the expiration date.

Options present an awesome opportunity to make money as long as the stock moves exactly like you want it to. If you buy a call option, the right to buy stock, we want the stock to go up. If it goes down or stays the same, we lose. Now ask yourself: Why am I buying this option when all the news has played out? At least ask, why did I buy the option with a near term expiration date? Maybe I should have bought the option with an expiration date at least into the next news reporting period.

Now all in all, observing this "news—no news" period should help us make wiser decisions. Decisions when to get in, decisions when to sell. Here is an important question: "What compelling reason does this stock have to go up?" More importantly, what compelling reason does this option have to go up in value? The answer is simple, but far-reaching. If there is nothing to drive it up—no news, no rumors, no nothing—then watch out.

Do you see where I now come up with "Red Light, Green Light?" A time to buy; a time *not* to buy. Now, notice I didn't say a time to sell. There are times when we should not be buying options. This goes back to a premise I've taught for years: the way to win at the stock market is to not lose! We need to avoid making mistakes. Buying a call option when a stock has nothing going on to help drive up the price is likely to be one of those mistakes.

1. There are no set dates on which all companies start announcing newsy things. The dates vary. They are different because the board may meet at odd times. After the board meets the company may still make no announcement for several days or even weeks.

2. Many companies make very few pre-announcements, if any at all. Some make a lot. These announcements start about two weeks before each company's particular quarter end. Often you'll hear, "Well, we're entering the earnings season," meaning that news is about to come out. Some people "get it" on this part of the whole process. What you'll never hear from TV and newspaper reporters is this: "Well, we're leaving the earnings reporting season."

Before I go on to (3), let me tell an interesting story: We were having our speaker training two-day session in March, actually the Ides of March (March 15) and the day after. It was in Seattle. We were discussing Microsoft. It's on everyone's mind in Seattle, as it's a Northwest company. There are news reports on it almost daily in our region.

The stock had been floundering from the middle of February through that time. I was explaining the "news–no news" concept to our instructors. After awhile, the subject of Microsoft came up. It was about 9 or 10 A.M. on Monday. I pointed out that the stock was down and had been stagnant for a few weeks. I said, "Microsoft needs March 15th. Oh, it is March 15th! So the news announcements should start soon."

The next morning, March 16th, the word on the street was that they were going to blow away their numbers—meaning they were making more money than expected. All in all the stock was up something like $7 to $8 in those two days. I looked at my great instructors and said, "Seeeeeeeeeee?"

It doesn't take a genius to figure out that if there's bad news, especially about earnings, or no news, the stock will go down. Anticipation and expectation of news reports play a big part of this game. If there's good news or rumors of good news, the stock reacts accordingly. The old expression, "No news is good news" is out the window here. It's the opposite now: "No news is bad news."

This leads up to number (3).

3. A lot of stock movement depends on the quality of the news. At the time of this writing our economy is picking up. Many companies are earning a lot of money. A few are struggling. My guess is that 30% of today's news is bad and about 70% is good. This will change.

   So with a lot of good news hitting the streets, why do some stocks go down? One answer is that many investors think they can't keep up this level of profits. Dell, for example, went up (had positive earnings announcements) many quarters in a row. One quarter they just hit their earnings estimates and the stock tanked. They're still a great company, earning millions, but some anticipate future sluggishness and the stock reacts. The marketplace is a giant auction. A stock goes for what someone will pay for it. Built into this are many factors, and one of the most important is anticipation of future earnings growth.

Check the quality of the news. Watch for news on one company and how it affects others in the same field. Observing this will let you see many buying and selling opportunities.

4. Not all companies follow the same exact time schedule. Many space out their announcements over a few days. Many make all of the news announcements at one time.

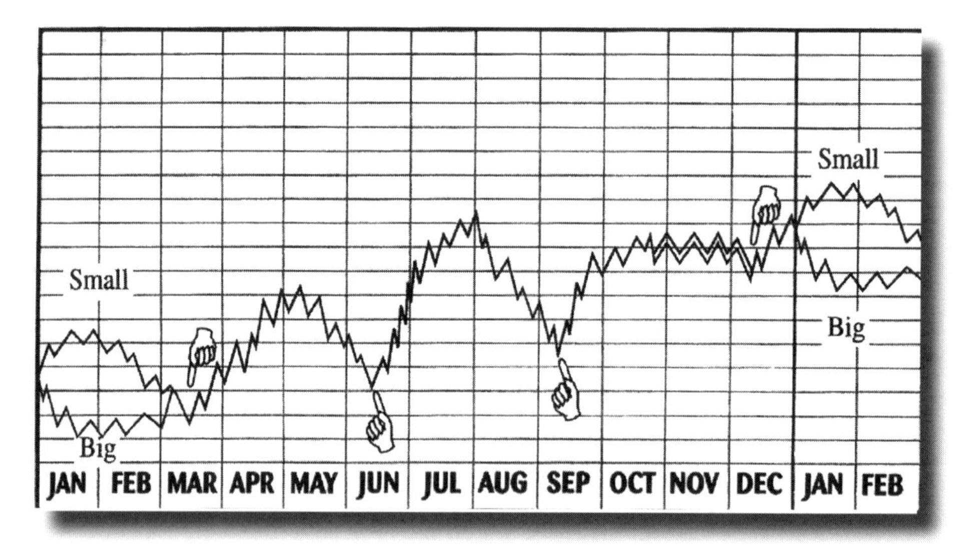

Look at the 14-month graph. Note, this is a generality. *Any particular* stock's movement is based on many things—certainly not just a chart in this book.

Observe:

1. The serious dips are in Feb, May, August, a neutral November and bad first two weeks of December.
2. October is a strange month with many erratic stock movements.
3. Look at the arrows. These represent the start of the news talk, the "green light" period.
4. The months following the year end are erratic because of the quality of the news, plus share buy-backs and stock splits.

SUMMARY

This chapter is about making better decisions, timing our entrance and exit points for more enhanced cash flow. The more dots we connect, the better it is for this process and the better for our bottom line. We also discussed the quantity and quality of news—how even the company's "anticipation of news" period drives a stock up or down. Option trades need movement in the right direction to be profitable. Before buying calls or puts, ask the all-important question: What compelling reason does the stock have to go up (or down for puts)? If you don't have a good answer, then refraining from trading straight options may be the best trade. This is another reason why I like writing covered calls. First, the stock price fluctuations create opportunity. Second, we can sell a call and put market forces (time and volatility) to work for us. Three, we're selling for cash now, not waiting and hoping for something to happen.

"Success comes from you, not to you."

Wade B. Cook

"You are not here merely to make a living. You are here to enable the world to live more amply, with greater vision, with a finer spirit of hope and achievement. You are here to enrich the world, but will lessen yourself if you forget the errand."

~Woodrow Wilson

"I committed myself to getting all of the education I could. I LOVE THIS STUFF! The best part of this, is the fact that I have been able to help my Mom and Dad retire in comfort (and lots of it) and I have been able to not worry about finances AT ALL! I plan on retiring in about 6 months, but probably sooner."

-Jason A., UT

"I have increased my faith promise to $1,000 per month for missions, and have been able to help some others whose needs were being challenged."

-Doug C., FL

"Bought a new home and now financing the upcoming birth of triplets."

-William S., GA

"I am excited about my future. I am 72 years old and have a new burst of energy. I have made over $250,000 in just 3 months selling covered calls and have definite plans to realize all my life's unfulfilled goals. What a rush!!"

-Dwight H., CA

CHAPTER TEN
WHAT CAN YOU DO TO MAKE MORE MONEY?
–YOU KNOW, THE LITTLE THINGS THAT MAKE BIG DIFFERENCES?

Yes, there are. I've found numerous strategies, techniques to aid the process of developing multiple rivers of income from writing covered calls. I've gathered these over years of trial and error.

1. **BUY-WRITE**

   A buy-write is a simple process your broker can use to buy the stock and sell the call simultaneously. You can often save 5-10 cents (maybe a little more). Why? There is a bid and ask on the stock purchase, and there is a bid and ask on the option sell. Example: The stock is $7.20 x $7.35. The $7.50 calls are going for .40 x .50. Typically you would buy at the ask of $7.35. Using our 1,000 share example, that's $7,350. We then sell the call at .40 (10 contracts) or $400. What if the broker/market makers would give up or chip in 5 or 10 cents—say buy the stock at $7.30, but still sell the call for .40. You save a nickel. That's $50 on 1000 shares.

   Buy-writes are not as common today as yesteryear. Remember the days of fractions? Stock at 7 3/8 x 7 ½; option at 3/8 x ½. The reason for changing to decimals was to tighten up the spread and save investors money. It worked. Sometimes there isn't that much extra to chip in.

2. **DRIPs are wonderful but . . .**

   DRIP stands for Dividend Re-Investment Program. Quite a few companies allow you, through your brokerage firm to use dividends to buy extra shares of stock. There is no commission on this. They (that's the invisible they—a trust arrangement) hold the money and once a quarter they go into the marketplace and purchase stock.

Small investors usually don't own that much stock so the dividend amount of .35 a share on 400 shares equals $140. The stock is at $59.40 so you will end up owning 402.6392 shares. Rarely will it come out even. You end up with fractional shares. Over the years this can add up to a lot of extra wealth. Think about it: the next quarter you have 402.6392 shares and the dividend is paid on the total shares you own. Soon you will have a decimal point with seven numbers after it.

What to do? Here are a few suggestions:

- My first reaction has been to participate in as many DRIPs as possible. Usually the companies that allow this are more solid. Since this book is about covered call writing, let's look at the consequences through that filter.

- Options are bought and sold in 100 share batches (unless there has been an odd stock split like a 3:2 or a 4:3). If you write a call on 413.739426 shares, you can still only write four contracts. And if you get called out you will sell the 400 shares and in your account will remain 13.739426 shares. If you don't want odd batches like this, don't participate in their DRIP program. You can choose whether or not to participate. You may decide to participate in only one DRIP on one stock, and opt to get the cash dividend on the others. If you do participate and end up with odd amounts of stock, you will still receive the annual shareholder report and can watch for developments in the company. Just remember that these reports and filings are expensive for the company to send out.

3. BUY STOCK IN 100 SHARE LOTS

For many people, the amount of shares of a stock to purchase is often determined by the amount of cash in the account. Doing it this way, an account could end up with 425 shares, or 590 shares of a stock. Pity. On 590 shares, we can only write 5 contracts. All that cash tied up in the 90 shares and we are left to the whims of the market forces of olden time—BCC, Before Covered Calls.

A way to fix this problem is to buy an extra ten shares when you can. Here's an assignment: Go through all of your stock positions, even in your IRA. Before you run out and buy up to the next one hundred share level, see how good of a covered call canidate the stock is. Measure rates of returns. In fact, check out the quality of the stock. I have a complete way to check out stocks—P/E ratios, debt, growth, etc.—in my book *Wade Cook's Stock Picking Handbook.* Here's a simple test to see if you should keep a stock, sell it or even buy more. Should I sell it is not a quality question. Here is a quality question: WOULD I BUY IT NOW? Your decision will be much better when you do the research to answer that question.

4. STOCK SPLITS

I've written on splits so often. My other books are full of information on the five times to play a stock split. For our purpose here we'll deal with purchasing stock headed into an off-beat split, such as a 3 for 2, or a 4 for 3 split. 3:2 splits are very common.

In a 3:2, if you have 200 shares, you'll end up with 300. 400 becomes 600, but 300 becomes 450. You will have left over shares when you write covered calls on 450 shares. If you already own stock you can decide to (a) leave it alone, (b) sell 50 shares, or (c) buy 50 shares. Check it out—do you want to own more shares?

If, however, you're contemplating buying a stock headed for a 3:2 split, consider buying 200 shares or 400 shares. In fact, any even one hundred share batch will end up okay. As of this writing I bought 200 shares of Bebe Stores (BEBE). In ten days it will end up as 300 shares. Also note, after a 3:2 split, the stock price goes down—Bebe Stores at $38 will go to $28 or so. The $40 calls will become the $28.625 calls. This stock will have odd strike prices until they expire – out 8 to 9 months.

The number of contracts stays the same, but each contract represents 150 shares. So, if I sold two contracts of the $40 calls before the split, I would end up with two contracts of the $28.625 calls, and each contract would control 150 shares.

A 4:3 means if you have 300 shares, you'll end up with 400 shares. Option contracts stay the same, except each contract equals 125 shares. You mathematicians can play with this for awhile.

5. **DON'T SELL ALL . . .**
If you own 1,000 shares of a $6.90 stock, you can sell six contracts of the $5 calls for $2.20 and four contracts of the $7.50 calls for 35 cents. You can sell 5 contracts of one strike price and leave 500 shares uncovered.

If you want to buy back a call, you don't have to buy back all of them. You could buy back six contracts and get called out of 400 shares.

6. **PENSION ACCOUNTS AND IRAs**
You can't do anything in an IRA that might require you to have to bring in more money. A purchase on margin might do that, and what if you've already made the maximum contribution for the year? Margin trading is forbidden in IRA accounts.

Covered call writing can become your job and add a lot of income. Hopefully, it will create a new tax problem for you. If you make $4,000 to $10,000 a month in an IRA, there are no taxes due until you take out the money.

Also note, as you get older you should train someone to do this for you. Isn't this one of the ways we win the game? And if you're going to make an IRA contribution, do it on January 2nd. Then you have an entire year of monthly cash flow—tax free currently.

7. **SELL THE LAST RUNUP IN THE STOCK PRICE.**
This is one of my favorites. Suppose you own, or want to buy, a pretty volatile stock. It moves from $10 to $9.50, and a few days later it's close to $12.

When it has a nice movement like this, why not sell the $10 calls? A question you must ask—"can the last rise in the stock be sustained?" If you think it can be sustained then don't sell the call right now. Wait and then sell the $10 call or even the $12.50 call. If you think it will give back a dollar or two of the last rise, selling the $10 call for, say $2.50, could be a winner.

The stock backs off to $10.50. The $10 call is going for $.70. You took in $2,500, spent $700—another cool $1,800 for a few days work. Oh, you're not working, you just put the market forces to work for you.

What if you owned this stock and saw it move from $12 back to $10.50? You hadn't read this book yet. It's BCC (Before Covered Calls). You'd be disappointed. Your stock went down. More complaining. But now that you've sold the $10 call for $2,500, you're cheering! Will it go down more? "Yeah. It's at $11.20. Come on baby, drop some more! Okay, whoa, $10.50. Yes, it's time to make the call." Ring Ring. "What are the $10 calls going for on XYZ stock? 70 cents? Okay, I want to place an order to buy back the $10 calls to close." $1,800 net, now we can afford a new fence.

Up or down, you're happy. If the stock stayed the same, you're glad. If the stock price goes down, you're glad and ready to buy back and sell again. If the stock goes up, you're happy too. You are profitable no matter what.

AUTHOR'S NOTE: I've seen many advertisements and seminars stating they'll show you how to make money in both up and down markets. Theory is one thing, real life is another. Oh sure, in up markets buy calls, in down markets buy puts. Easy? HA!

Just ask to see their personal trades. Have them put their trades out for the whole world to see. That's what I ask them. They won't do it. Tell them "Wade Cook does! Wade Cook puts it all out there for the whole world to see!"

By the way, you just saw a trade in a down stock and we made $1,800, still own the stock and we're poised to make more.

"EVERYONE'S A GENIUS IN A BULL MARKET."
~Wade Cook

8. YOU AND ME

I'm in this for the long haul. My career is my hobby and my hobby is my career. I live a charmed life. I love to teach—mostly Bible lessons—but next is teaching people ways to live a more quality financial life.

Today's Money Changers are . . . well, you figure it out. Log on, attend an event. Most of my events are on the phone—teleconferences. You can learn at home, trade at home, and be with your kids and grandkids. Maybe someday my kids will teach your grandkids, or vice-versa.

My passion is to help others. Let's go down this road together.

CHAPTER ELEVEN
RE-ALLOCATE YOUR ASSETS

There is no proof like the proof of something that really works. You've heard that "the proof is in the pudding." Every section in this book has given you pudding—chocolate, coconut cream, bread pudding, even tapioca. Every stock has good and bad points. Every strategy for selling options has good and better times. It's not a matter of "if you'll make money"—but how much and how often.

My original reason for writing this book still stands. I want to help as many people as I can develop assets that produce a never ending stream of cash flow. This is financial independence at its very best. Once you know the basics you have the independence to develop even greater skills. You'll have the independence to work more or keep your schedule part time. You'll have freedom from financial stress.

Your assets can keep growing and now you know how. You'll have assets producing monthly income for paying the bills now and an income source and stream that can and should outlive you.

Do you know how to win? If you know and use the "how-to's" of covered call writing you will win several times a month. These skills can be transmitted easily to family, friends and employees. You can stay with it yourself or have others take over. You don't have to worry about the small amounts of income social security and a pension provide. The power is in your hands to change your life financially and do much good in the world.

"Do well, so you can do good"

~Wade Cook

<u>You</u> can do it! You can do it <u>now</u>! You can do it <u>here</u>! I've tried to convince you of this throughout this book. Examples have been real trades. Profits are real. Rates of returns—either as a percentage or real cash on cash returns—are achievable in a step by step process.

Many, however, still do not get it. I hear, "If I only had a million dollars." It's as if some mystical, magical amount will make everything okay. No, wealth creation and cash flow generation are a set of skills that few are born with. They are learnable skills. Read this quote from Henry Ford:

> *"If money is your hope for independence you will never have it. The only real security that a man (or woman) will have in this world is a reserve of knowledge, experience and ability."*

Money is the product of a process. For years I've told people to think backwards, or inside out, or whatever…

With covered calls, I'm not saying that. You need to tweak what you're already doing. You need to add a few insights and skills to your existing formulation. "Knowledge, experience and ability" to look carefully at existing assets: cars, real estate, bank accounts, stocks, jewelry, etc. and ask:

1. Are these appreciating assets or are they depreciating in value?
2. Are they generating income or costing income (expense)?
3. Can I re-allocate part of these and use them for income purposes?

Even $20,000 in tied up, restricted assets can produce $3,000 to $5,000 per month. You can make a nice car payment with $4,000 per month. Many people can pay off a $200,000 mortgage in two or three years at this rate.

There's a better life waiting and there isn't much standing in the way. Your ship may be safe in the harbor, but that's not what ships are for. Set sail.

Another metaphor from the sea: "The biggest fish you'll ever catch is still swimming in the ocean." My job as an educator is to show you how to choose a worthy boat, find the right place to fish, and stay at it longer. The world is now your oyster.

LET ME CRITIQUE MYSELF

May I take a wild step and critique my own efforts in this book to educate you. I will ask myself some questions:

Q1: Have I stated clearly my objectives?

A: Yes, to a large extent, but there will still be many who question my intentions. One time, in Philadelphia on a radio show, a caller asked, "If you're making so much money, why are you out here teaching?" All I said was, "Sir, I can tell you've never been a teacher. My love for sharing is unsurpassed."

A2: My objectives are to show you one clear, concise method for building up assets to produce monthly income.

Q2: Have I given specific knowledge in a usable way?

A: I've used dozens of examples to facilitate the learning process. Repetition is the best teacher. My only regret is that many will still say, "Okay, you can do it, what about me?" They will date this book and say, "It can't be done now!" I sincerely hope you'll join me online and see the deals done all of the time. I did real covered calls ten years ago for a book. I did them here, and I'll be doing them in the future, side-by-side with you ten years from now.

A2: I've used real trades. I've used trades in different price ranges. I've used different amounts of start up money to include everyone. One reason for real examples (especially using arithmetic) is that you can read over them many times—until you "get it". And believe me, "getting it" is definitely worth it.

Q3: What would I do differently in writing this book?

A: I would probably give more actual verbiage in how to talk (place a trade) with your broker. However, I've given a lot. One reason I didn't do more of this is because so many people are now trading online.

A2: I might have solicited more actual student transactions, but time is important and I've done so many trades on my own.

Q4: Is there one last thing you would like to share about covered calls?

A: Yes: Don't let uncertainty stop you. The learning curve is not that tough to get through. There are many nay-sayers. Don't let anyone stop you.

It is so easy to be negative and sarcastic. It takes a winner to keep thinking right, planning right, and to do positive things. So, here's the point: if money were not an issue—what would your life be like? How much good could you do? The answer to this is the reason covered call writing is so important! It is the freedom that only covered call writing can give.

With that, let me reverse this Q&A and ask my dear readers one final question: "What is God doing in your life?"

BONUS CHAPTER
TEN INDISPUTABLE AND OFTEN GUT-WRENCHING RULES OF FINANCIAL SUCCESS

"For every person wishing to teach
there are thirty not wanting to be taught."

~W.C. Sellar (1898-1951)
British humorous writer.

Let's explore the ramifications of the above statement. First, I sure hope you're not one of the thirty. That's a dead end street. I think most people realize the value of education. They know that highly educated individuals are usually highly paid. The difference between someone making $60,000 a year and someone making $260,000 is attributable to knowledge—more specifically, the proper application of knowledge.

Proof is all around us that the above statement about knowledge is true. Why is it, then, that most people cut short their progress and dampen their future potential by cutting short the educational process? Here's another question: we all know experience is the best teacher—then why don't we more completely add to our repertoire of learning methods the wisdom gained from the experiences of others?

The results of this inadequate way of thinking are magnified in the financial arena. Think about it. Everything you have learned to do and to do well you were hand-trained by someone else. You didn't learn to drive a car by reading a drivers-ed manual. It would be foolish to think a seventeen year old boy could be a championship level high school quarterback without proper coaching and visual examples, not to mention the hours of practice and drills. Why is it, then, that when it comes to financial matters, we think we can read a book, check the newspaper once in awhile, or, the silliest of all: trust a commissioned based stockbroker, who gets paid to sell investments, and then wonder why we get such poor results?

I want you to pause and think about these important aspects of wealth accumulation and cash flow enhancement. Your results will be in direct proportion to how well you learn and apply the following ten rules.

How a "Street Smart" Cab Driver Took On Wall Street and Won Big!
I want to be America's premier financial strategist. I will teach you all my secrets for getting rich and staying rich despite the economy or today's tax laws.

I was a taxi cab driver in the '70s. Borrowing $500 from my father, I started buying real estate. My innovative ideas and follow-through enabled me to turn that $500 into several million. But that's nothing compared to what I'm doing on Wall Street. Starting with little, using my "Rolling Stock", "Stock Split" and "Covered Call" methods, I've show students how to create extra income. I'm not smarter than the next guy, but I am "street smart." What I discovered while driving a cab changed my life forever.

While my fellow cabbies were out looking for the big runs, I took every little run I could find. $4 here, $5 there. You see, it costs $1.50 just to get into a cab (something called a meter drop) even if you only go two blocks. At the end of a month, and by doing numerous small runs (the ones other cab drivers ignored) I made three times what they made.

I apply this "meter drop™" technique to my stock market investment business—netting money on a lot of little trades, rather than risking everything on one or two big ones. I developed a unique system for investing that "treats investing in the stock market like a business." I have written over 20 books. One of them, *Wall Street Money Machine*, reached #3 on the New York Times Business Best-Seller List. I have appeared on 1,600 radio and TV stations, and even today with my Team Wall Street Staff present two-day Wall Street Workshops across America.

As I move through these ten rules in this special report, I would like to introduce you to my amazing home/car study course about the stock market and so much more. It's called Stock Market Accelerated Returns Training (SMART). A few questions to set the stage:

- How would you like to meet someone who has made millions—literally cash flow millions—in the market?

- What if you found that many of these profits were made in numerous small $1,000 and $2,000 transactions?

- How difficult has it been for you to find someone, anyone, who will teach you tried and proven methods to generate income, wealth or any type of financial success?

- Would you like to spend time with (learn from) someone who gets nothing out of what you do? Would you like to look over the shoulder of a millionaire and watch money being made?

- Would you like to learn from a pure educator—someone who is a student first, a teacher second—and who has no investments for sale?

- Would you like that someone to be accepted by, even ignored by the so- called pool of financial professionals, or would you like that someone to be a leader in new and unique ways and then be slammed by criticism from the status quo pros?

In all of this you will find me, Wade Cook. I am a taxicab driver turned "meter drop™" cash flow specialist. I walk the walk. I love teaching and will share with you little known ways to make potential big bucks. I will uncover for you the hidden secrets of the truly rich and let you share in the enterprise. Yes, I have become the most controversial man in America. I'm happy with this. Who wants boring, stodgy, risky and gambling type investments? I'm about safety, cash flow and "treating the stock market like a business." No wonder the big guys on Wall Street hate me so. I am such a threat to their “get the commission at any cost” way of life.

Tens of thousands of students have benefited greatly from following these “down-in-the-trenches" cash flow formulas. All of this has now been put together in a comprehensive home study course of audio CDs and manuals called SMART (Stock Market Accelerated Return Training). Do you want a leg up on the tired and weak investments being foisted on Americans? Then you need to hear me out in this SMART course. Do you want to be cash flow consistent, rather than being sold some hot "investment du jour?" If so, SMART is a must. Do you want to know what retail stockbrokers know, or do you want to know the details of what billion dollar traders know and do? I expose all in this handsomely packaged mega-course on stock market income formulas. And last, do you want complicated education that takes years to master, if even then? If you do, you will have to go somewhere else, because SMART is easy-to-follow, easy-to-understand, and uses easy-to-implement methods and techniques. It's taught in a lively format of real examples, great explanations, functional demonstrations and presentations. SMART has beautiful manuals with documentation, examples and add-on materials. So, whether you learn best by seeing, hearing or reading, this important information is delivered so you can grasp it, comprehend it and use it TODAY: “When the student is ready the teacher appears. " Are you ready?

“Humans always have fear of an unknown situation—this is normal. The important thing is what we do about it. If fear is permitted to become a paralyzing thing that interferes with proper action, then it is harmful. The best antidote to fear is to know all we can about a situation.”

~John Glenn, Jr.

I started this chapter off with a quote about 30 people not wanting to learn. I hope what you read in the following ten rules convinces you to not take on the losing attitude of those 30 people. There’s simply too much at stake for you, and I want to help you achieve your own great success.

INDISPUTABLE RULE #1:
WALK WITH PEOPLE OF WISDOM AND EXPERIENCE

"He that walketh with wise men shall be wise"

~Proverbs 13:20

I stood in front of a class one day and asked a very simple, yet far-reaching question: "How many of you want to make at least $100,000 per year? Almost everyone raised their hands. I continued, "Then why are you talking to anyone about making money who is making less than $100,000 per year? To whom are you listening?"

The point I was making is that most people giving advice and selling investments, "ain't making no money." I proceeded to show the people several ideas that could make them over $100,000 and commented that many of the attendees go home and have these methods shot down by people making less than $50,000. I have put a few testimonials below this copy; so you can see some of my students in action.

It's sad to think of the others who have let small-minded people belittle their attempts to gain wealth and better their family's financial situation.

Keep away from people who try to belittle your ambitions. Small people always do that, but the really great make you feel that you too can become great.

~ Mark Twain

What if these people had listened to negative comments?

Increased my account value from $25,000 to $160,000 in eight months.
~Calis A. , CA

I have made $150,000 this year so far in Options—Covered Calls and Puts.
~Bijan I, TX

Oh, I have had my fair share of critics, and criticism by people who have never read my books or attended my seminars: However, look at what these two wise financial professionals say:

I had some experience with options ~because I had worked on the Commodity Exchange in New York (COMEX). This workshop taught me so much more about using options & stocks. I think this is great, I just wish that I had heard of this 10 years ago. I would be up front in the class teaching to everyone else. Thanks.

~Dave R., NJ

I have 25 years experience as a broker with 3 major firms, and I was convinced I had nothing to learn from Wade Cook. How wrong I was! It was the most professional, dynamic, and thoroughly enjoyable series of meetings I have ever attended. I plan to write my clients and advise them to seriously consider attending the next seminar that is scheduled. Once again, it was a profoundly educational seminar.

~Carl G., CO

In fact, I could let these professionals and other students write this whole chapter. You see, they're doing it. They are now walking the walk. They're making it cash flow BIG. Read these next three testimonials and then I'll pose a question.

I've made $1,338,081.43 net profit in 11 1/2 months. I originally started with $36,000.

~Myke I., WA

I had $36,000 and turned it into $460,000 in less than 3 months. In another account, I took $100,000 and turned it into $400,000 in 4 weeks, and in another, I made $30,000 in 1 week for a total (account balance) of $960,000.

~John T., OK

I started trading on 10-19-95 with $2,900. ..I recently took an account from $16,000 to $330,000 in 2 weeks, and $35,000 to $2,484,000 in 6 weeks. I made ~1.25million in one day.

~Glenn M., IL

Is there anyone in your life that can help you take $36,000 and make $1,338,000 in 11 ½ months? I doubt you have someone who knows how. Can your stockbroker show you how to make $960,000 a year—starting with $136,000? I seriously doubt It. And the funny thing is that he or she is the one who needs to come up to speed and quit criticizing that which they do not know and do not understand. It must be easier to bad mouth and criticize than to learn and change.

"Genius has always had violent opposition from mediocre minds."

~Albert Einstein

But, now you have a clear choice. Do you stay with the old, worn out, outdated and risky ways or move up a couple of notches to successful, time-honored and street-tested methods? In every business, in every sport, in every field there are always people who excel, people who are a cut above, people who get better results. It seems like the deck is stacked in their favor. Success is not really that complicated. It's knowing your target and direction; setting priorities, being "that type" of person and good old fashioned coaching—again, to whom are you listening? How would you like to sit at the feet of a cash flow expert with your $5,000, $50,000 or $500,000 for over 20 hours, and then be able to repetitiously learn, refresh yourself; check on and keep going with seven incredible ways to cash flow the market? I am that income expert and SMART could be your path to wealth.

"Develop a passion for learning. If you do, you will never cease to grow."

~Anthony J. D'Angelo

INDISPUTABLE RULE #2: PASSION, PRECISION—THEN PROFITS

There absolutely will not be success without energy, dedication and passion. Passion for away of life, a cause or goal is an unmistakable and often overlooked element of success. But passion is sine qua non, an indispensable condition, to the process. Without passion, one will not stick with the process long enough to gain the expertise and knowledge of the details, the precise methods needed to succeed.

The stock market is no different than any other business, endeavor or pursuit. The market has methods of failure and methods of success. It has strategies for long-term growth and strategies for generating income now. Most people I've met don't have millions of dollars. You'd swear by listening to the financial TV shows and by reading the magazines that they view everyone as having ten million dollars to play around with. But, what about the little guys? Who is there for them? Most stockbrokers sell you investments for the future—way out there when they won't have to be responsible for the results. I teach you how to income trade for the good old here and now.

I am not about "asset allocation"—a clear mark of an elitist snob, but about "formula allocation" and making the stock market produce actual monthly income so my students can quit their jobs, payoff debts and support their families. So what does this mean to you? Well, let's look at how we use passion to gain the precision that will result in steady profits.

I have discovered seven fantastic income formulas. The word "income" in the last sentence needs to be emphasized. I'm not talking about growth or tax deductions, but actual cash. Cash (checks) you can have in the mailbox in a few days—or drop by and pick up in an hour or so. It's $2,000 from buying 1,000 shares of a stock for $1.50, or $1,500, and having it roll up to $3.75 and then selling it for $3,750—pocketing $2,000 after commissions.

This is Rolling Stock—one of my 7 Income Formulas. Rolling Stock is a stock you've a watched, from three types of patterns (which you'll learn to recognize in SMART). You can practice trade, place GTC orders and get out with profits and with a minimum of risk. Yes--knowledge (tracking) brings the risk way down. This formula has a beginning, a middle, and an end. It has stop-out points to stop excess losses if it moves wrong. It is based on technica1s. There are learnable details that can be copied again and again. That's what a formula is—a pattern of success. Formulas like this let you help build success in the other (family, spiritual, etc.) areas of your life.

"I just wanted to let you know, that I was able to play one rolling stock over a three week period, seven times, and was able to realize a $7,500 profit from a $500   investment."

~Thom A, UT

Can your stockbroker help you take $500 and make $7,000 in three weeks? I don't think so. You could check me out on this. Ask a stockbroker to take $500 and make $7,500, or show you any time where they've done this in the past. Tell them Wade Cook can show me, and they can see all of my trades at www.wadecook.org.

Many people lack the passion necessary to succeed because they don't know what's out here. If you have never seen baseball played, or never played catch, how would you know if you like baseball or not? And how would you knw if you like baseball well enough to get good at it?

In this regard, the course, SMART, stands alone—setting new standards in education. At the same time the materials explain and explore the methods to show you why they will work for you, while simultaneously showing you how they work-the exact, precise formulas for profits.

In short, don't expect continued profit without first having a certain level of passion and second, acquiring the expertise to succeed. Otherwise, the third step, the results or the profits will never come.

Before I go on, I want to include a few insights into common characteristics of great people. I wrote a book called Success: American Style. Writing this book started me thinking about common threads in the lives of great people. I noticed several things that definitely were "bridges of commonality" among truly great men and women in this country. Let me give you a quick list of those observations.

1. Almost every great person whom I have observed and studied had, if not a passionate love for God, at least a reverence for the finer things in life, meaning in this instance, the spiritual side of life. This side of life is not only important to them, but it is openly apparent.

2. I saw that almost all great people were very active in the lives of their family and friends. If their families were not involved in their businesses or their careers, at least they were involved in major portions of their life. One of the things I have consistently observed in our Wall Street Workshop graduates is they usually come up and tell me their stories in twos and threes; families, husbands and wives, or fathers and mothers with their kids. The most excited ones were trading together, in a group with their family or friends.

3. The next thing I observed in the lives of truly great people was that they took control of their own education. Nobody had to tell them to get educated. Can you imagine Abraham Lincoln being scolded by his mother for not studying late at night in front of the fire? Can you imagine George Washington Carver, or Thomas Sowell, or any of the other great leaders of our country in that scenario? They were a step ahead of virtually everyone else, by knowing what their education was going to do for them. They knew where they wanted to be, and they knew wisdom and the proper application of knowledge bring good results.

4. Every great person I have studied had a passion for excellence. They knew that winning in life or being successful in any

business enterprise means dealing with the details--and as I've said in many of my seminars recently; you need the three "Ps": Passion, Precision, and then the Profits. There are a lot of people that want profits without the passion and the precision. What I've tried to do with these audio seminars and video presentations is to make sure you have this information in a ready-when-you-need-it format

5. I've also noticed in reading about and studying these extraordinary people is that they have a tremendous love for all people—specifically those they were working with and those around them. This love is manifested in their actions. The point is, they are part of a whole; they can do great things, but they also want to share those great things and have the people around them also doing great things and share in the blessings.

INDISPUTABLE RULE #3: BLENDING BENEFITS OF OWNERSHIP

There are three benefits of owning any financial investment. One of the primary reasons why people own investments is for the income it will produce, now or in the future. Another reason for ownership is the tax benefits: deductions, expenses, credits and other write-offs. The third reason for owning investments is future growth—an increase in value.

Again, cash flow, tax write-offs and growth. If you had to pick one, which would it be? Is there a way to get all three with the same investment? Where should you put your emphasis? These are all great questions. Let's explore them.

Most people who attend my seminars and buy my books are looking for cash flow; they figure they can buy all the boring investments they need later. For now, they need income to raise a family, pay the bills and not be tied down working for someone else.

Let's not leave this thought process. I realized early in my educational career-over two decades ago—that people need more income. My first publisher said, "Wade, we've got dozens of books on how to make millions, can you write us a book on how to make a living?" I picked up on this, and this idea has been the theme of my seminars, workshops and books. Others agree. Read these student's comments about monthly income. Read between the lines what these people can do with this new found cash flow that does not require an 8 to 5 job.

Just using the few strategies I've tried I'm now trading full time and have averaged $10,000 per month in profits over the past six months.

~Don B., CA

I am averaging $30,000/month on spreads and call options.

~Edward A., HI

Average $18,000 per month with mostly Covered Calls for the past 7 months.

~Gary B., TN

Okay, so they now make good money, how do they protect it? Can we blend all three benefits? It's tough with just one format, i.e. the stock market, to get cash flow, tax write-offs and growth simultaneously. With real estate and with owning your own business it's much easier. That's why my books, *Real Estate Money Machine*, *How to Pick Up Foreclosures* and *101 Ways to Buy Real Estate Without Cash* have continued to sell in bookstores so well. Note: *101 Ways* was given a "10 out of 10" by Robert Bruss, the syndicated columnist.

I have been about cash flow for years. I have a constant theme. Here it is: BUILD UP A GROUP OF ASSETS TO PRODUCE THE INCOME YOU NEED TO LIVE ON. Most people work for someone else. They trade their time (expertise) for money. This is FICA type income, even if it's made in their own business. Wise people slowly but consistently put aside money into investments that produce unearned income (i.e. no Social Security taxes). Wouldn't it be great to eventually (say in 9 months to 2 years) have enough of this type of income to live on? How about this: get your money to work even harder than you do—with real cash flow paycheck results. If you don't order SMART right away, the battle will be too tough to win on your own. Oh, you can be successful, but why not leapfrog your way to wealth? You can avoid all the costly mistakes I've made. Remember it's truly a wise person who learns from the experience of others.

I started with $380 using Wades strategies buying calls on slams, buying calls m stock splits, buying stocks and writing covered calls. I have increased my portfolio to over $25,000. ~Jeff N, MO

One way to list these cash flow formulas is to graphically place them side by side with what the professionals in the industry help their clients do. We realize this is embarrassing for them. They work hard at selling things—it's a shame they don't know of these other methods—or at least don't show us these ways to make money! It seems they don't want us to know these techniques.

Here is a basic breakdown of the differences between "financial professional's methods" and my formulas. The only gut-wrenching aspect to this is that so many Americans get caught up in a dependency on these people, and never learn and apply these strategies themselves.

Yes, we are different:
The following shows the major difference between Liberty Network, Inc and all the other financial professionals.

Professionals	Liberty Network, Inc.
1.They receive commissions for selling investments, regardless of returns to client.	1.We sell no investments. We get nothing out of what you do.
2.They advise clients of specific investments.	2.We explain formulas, methods, and techniques to work the market. Stocks are mentioned as working examples. No specific advice is given.
3.Many financial professionals get paid a percentage of the asset base they manage, whether assets increase or decrease.	3.We teach. The students learn and earn. They work the formulas, after paper or simu-trading, and keep all the profits.
4.They sometimes get investors involved in risky investments	4.We show students how to avoid and minimize risk with a dedication to knowledge and specific tools like low-cost options, spreads, and writing covered calls.
5.They preach "asset allocation" placing portions of investor's money in harms way.	5.We teach "formula allocation" for cash flow, tax write-offs, and growth. We help students learn to find certain stocks/options that fit the formulas.
6.They constantly sell investors the new "investment du jour."	6.We teach and show investors how to work the formulas, spread out risk, avoid losses and not get caught up in erractic and fad investments.
7.Most do not show their trading results, they surely do not publicize their personal trades.	7.We tell, show, and do all. All trades are listed on our internet site at www.wadecook.org.

And now from one of our students:

"After learning of the strategies last August, I began doing some rolling stock and covered calls. These small trades worked like they were supposed to, then I listened to my broker and was swayed from the formulas. Soon after, I was over my head and lost a great deal of money. Wade made me realize how important it is to get good at the very basic strategies and not to listen to a stockbroker selling his agenda."

~Peter C, MO

INDISPUTABLE RULE #4: EXPERIENCE IS THE BEST TEACHER, BUT…

People do some pretty strange things to get educated. There's the traditional school/college format. Some use home school. There's OJT, or On the Job Training. Many corporations and the military use this method. Many very successful people are self-taught. Some people get by on as little education as possible, while others never quit learning. Today; many use the Internet and other computer retrieval systems as a research library.

There is a truth among successful people which cannot be set aside: it is that they take education seriously. Not one great person I've met disparaged knowledge. Indeed, acquiring knowledge and wisdom is their way of life. The thought of being consistently dedicated to acquiring education may be gut wrenching to some, but tremendously exciting to others. Here are additional items to help keep this in perspective and focus attention on this important rule of success.

(A) Stay a step ahead by knowing what your education will do for you. Get educated to get results.
(B) Become a career student. Albert Einstein at the age of 74 said, "I'm engaged in the study of Physics." Check out the word "engaged."
(C) Get to be an expert at something. Don't quit your educational process short of success. One student, a race car driver, said,

"you don't want to be going 150 miles an hour into a turn and run out of knowledge."

(D) No one can learn and know everything. Be around the best teachers and educated minds, you can find.

(E) Use the wisdom gained from the experiences of others. Yes, experience is the best teacher, but it's so very expensive. With all of this as a road map, I have created the SMART Study Course. It's fun, it's powerful, and it will help you get better results. I'd love to be on your team.

"Experience is a hard teacher;
because she gives the test first, the lesson after."

~Vernon Law

INDISPUTABLE RULE #5
THE SKILLS OF KEEPING WEALTH ARE DIFFERENT THAN THE SKILLS OF BUILDING WEALTH

Many business builders have a Genghis Khan mentality. They conquer territory; then conquer some more. Then, while they plunder and pillage the next country; they put inept administrators in the previously conquered lands, and then almost as quickly as the empire was built, it collapses. Managing requires different skills than conquering.

I learned this lesson the hard way. In fact, I'm so thickheaded, I've had to learn it a few times. I came to know of letter E in Rule #4 about learning from the experiences of others the hard way. And you also must learn this rule. I hope you don't have to learn it the hard way.

You can build up a nice set of assets or build a business quickly, but the mindset and efforts to build and acquire is totally different than the mindset and efforts needed to keep, maintain and protect your assets.

Many people stay in the acquisition mode (conquering) and never transition to the far more difficult role of maintenance. The stock market is rife with companies following this pattern. You'll learn about these investing methods in SMART, however, this report is not about these nearsighted companies, but about you personally.

Here are some thoughts:

(A) Learn more details. Work to be an expert at your chosen topic. Use what you know about your business to explore other investment opportunities.
(B) Don't get caught in the "make it in ours, lose it in theirs" merry-go-round.
(C) Keep your investments (business interests) so you can list all of them on one piece of paper. Keep your management chores simple. Peace in simplicity.
(D) Build upon what you know. I teach a simple concept in regards to Rolling Stock, Writing Covered Calls, Spreads and Stock Splits; it's called, "Know your exit before you ever go in the entrance." Why is this exit strategy important in this discussion? Because, with your business or investments you'll do one of three things to exit:

    (1) Stay and run it forever.
    (2) Hire someone to manage it for you.
    (3) Sell the business.

(E) This passion, this dedication to accomplishment creates and perpetuates a certain optimism that is contagious.

If you know what the end game will be, you'll make better decisions daily to achieve the results you want.

What's more important: acquiring or retaining? Focus your education on the results you want. Example: I'm under no I delusion that some people will purchase the SMART course and attend my awesome 2-day Wall Street Workshop, and then change careers and become a "Stock Market Trader." Don't get me wrong, thousands have. They live off the income. Trading, not investing, becomes the "horse to ride on"—see Rule #10. It's wonderful to read their stories, BUT it's more common to have people increase their trading ability and generate a little more income so they can start a different business, or keep extra ~ money to go into their chosen profession. I want to help people improve the quality of their life, not completely change it. It's amazing what an extra $5,000 or $10,000 a month can do. Again, some use this new knowledge to completely change their lives, others use it to tweak and improve what they're already doing.

INDISPUTABLE RULE #6:
WEALTH HAS THREE ENEMIES

We work so hard to support our families. If possible we squeak out a little to start investing. We try a few business ideas and finally after 10 to 15 years we become an "overnight" success. But success has additional price tags.

There are three financial Goliaths out and about. Three problems that can destroy our wealth; and if not completely destroy it, at least, curtail it. These financial behemoths are: (1) lawsuits, (2) income taxes and (3) death taxes. These three can come at anytime and they can come in different forms.

There is a solution for all three of these problems and solving them is easier than you think. I'll help you see it with a few questions:

Question #1: If you make all of the money you make under you (or 'you plural' as a husband and wife), will everything be taxed in one higher tax bracket? Even if you set up one family corporation, and make all of your money there, is it all taxed in one bracket?

Question #2: If you own all of your assets in one entity, say under you or in joint tenancy (the most dangerous form of ownership between a husband and wife) with your spouse, could one lawsuit wipe out everything, and will you have one tax situation for a large estate on your death?

The solution to both of these problems is to split up your assets. Do not own everything in one legal entity. You need to understand and use

Corporations, Limited Partnerships, Living Trusts, and Pension Trusts. These four domestic entities are awesome when blended together. Probably everyone reading right now needs at least two of them. Look at what this financial professional had to say about the knowledge he gained at a Wade Cook event:

As a former financial planner, I thought I knew a lot about securities and the market. As a current attorney I thought I knew a lot about companies and securities. Now I know I knew nothing about companies, securities, and the market.

~Michael R, WA

You need these tools to acquire and maintain your wealth in a healthy manner.

INDISPUTABLE RULE #7: BIG RESULTS FROM SMALL THINGS

OR: The Bottom Line Key to Wealth is Repetition & Duplication.

Even God didn't create the earth in one day. The rule for progress is, line upon line, precept upon precept. Yet all around I see people trying to get rich fast. Wealth is best built slowly; Even cash flow can be built up. Not many people all of a sudden need $20,000 a month to live on.

Most people at first need an extra $1,000 or $2,000 to pay some bills. Then they need to replace the income from their job so they can spend their time with their family; or go back to school, or travel. Most of us want and need steady income. That suits me just fine. For years my books and seminars have been about using a "meter drop" method—small, repeatable profits. Repetition and Duplication, doing lay-ups every day is the secret to wealth creation.

"Victory is not won in miles but in inches. Win a little now, hold your ground, and later win a little more."

~ Louis L'Amour

How dare I think I can help someone make $50,000 if I can't first help them make $5,000 a month consistently. Sufficient cash flow, and then later on, excess cash flow, lets you live the lifestyle you want. Cash flow will make your financial world go round.

Small, repeatable profits. Know what you want from each trade. Choose a style of trading that generates the benefit you want. Find a trading style that fits a quality lifestyle—not the other way around. Learn, practice, understand, practice some more, go for results and persevere, stick to it and keep going—in small steps, a thousand here, a thousand there. Soon we'll be talking about real money. The one gut-wrenching lesson from this rule will come when you bite off more than you can chew. Don't get "big-deal-it is."

INDISPUTABLE RULE #8:
THE ONLY CONSTANT IS CHANGE:
STICK OUT, DO GREAT THINGS

You note that a constant theme of all my stock market books is to put market forces to work for you. There is one, and only one, consistent truth in the stock market. Here it is: "STOCK PRICES FLUCTUATE." Harness and put to work these fluctuations. This is why writing covered calls is such a powerful way to make money. Recently, I read this quotation: "Trust Movement." It says so much. Nothing stays the same. Everything is improving or decaying. Because of change, Rule #4 (EXPERIENCE IS THE BEST TEACHER) takes on added significance—keep learning, keep improving: "If it ain't broke, fix it anyway; " Not only should we live life with an attitude of gratitude, but an attitude of amplitude: living the laws of abundance and magnifying that which we've been given.

There is no happiness in mediocrity. There is happiness in growth, in new challenges--in creating something. Malcolm Forbes said, "No success is ever accomplished by a reasonable man." J. Paul Getty, the famous billionaire said, "No one can possibly achieve any real and lasting success or "get rich" in business by being a conformist."

Great people have a passion for that which is real. They have a passion for improvement. They have a need to make things better. Money is not the cause, but the effect of an attitude and action. We reap what we sow.

A question I've frequently asked audiences is this: if the next five years of your financial life are a mirror of the last five years, where will you be? Pretty much, where you are. Don't expect great things without doing great things. Don't expect results different from what your actions dictate. Read and think about this quote from the great Physicist, Albert Einstein, "The same thinking that got us into this mess will not get us out." Don't expect your circumstances to change without you changing first.

Financial strength allows people to be better at doing good. Winners focus on the finish line. They count the cost, determine the course and win, not because they are good starters, but because they are good finishers.

My life now is enriched by my ability to give more of my time and myself I spend many quality hours with my family that, before becoming a full time stock trader; were spent at the office, or traveling. The second is chairing a fund raising event fir the charitable organization People Reaching Out (PRO). PRO is dedicated to caring of teenagers and ~ their families that have been affected by alcohol drugs, or violence. My new life is a blessing that I treat with great respect and caring. –Ted N, CA

I just gave a check for $3, 000 to my church to pay off a building loan.

-Harley S., OH

Daughter needed an operation that insurance would not cover: Started with $4,500, the operation was $5,200. Still have $5,000 after the operation. Now making $400 car payment.

-Jim L., OK

I'll end this with a quotation from one of my students: "When the fear of staying the same is greater than the fear of change, we will change."

INDISPUTABLE RULE #9: FOCUS ON THE PRICE (PROCESS), NOT ON THE PRIZE

"The quality of a person's life is in direct proportion to their commitment to excellence, regardless of their chosen field of endeavor."

~ Vince Lombardi

I have been a student of people. I wonder all the time why it is that some people make it while others don't. I've seen people attend my events—paying thousands of dollars and going home afterward to put what they've learned into practice. One person starts with $5,000 and makes $11,600. Another person starts with the same $5,000, and makes $60,000.

"In just under thirty days my brokerage account had gone from $5,000 to a whopping $11,600."

~L-Robert H, WA

"I took $5,000 and made about $60,000 by December 31st."

~Missy S., NC

What's the difference? Why do so many Americans end up dead broke at age 65 when we live in such a great country full of opportunity and freedom?

I've come to two conclusions:

(1) Most people are not willing to pay the price of success. I've often said: "Some people think there is a wealth trade-off: they think they can trade being poor for being rich. There is no such trade. You do not trade being poor for being rich you trade being poor for being <u>on the road</u> to being rich. And being on the road to being rich is much harder than being poor."

(2) Most people do not get rich simply because they do not deserve it. What knowledge have they gained, what experiences have they had, that qualify them to get rich?

In all I've done as an educator, my mission has been to build up people to give them hope; and then give specific ways to build and keep wealth. It all starts with increasing basic monthly income.

Let me share with you what this means. If you want me to learn and then explain what a typical stockbroker, making $40-$60,000 a year knows, or a myopic financial planner with his $2,000 computerized estate plan ("You need more life insurance and you need to buy these mutual funds"); or if you need me to regurgitate what $50-$75,000 financial journalists spew forth as financial wisdom, you'll be sorely disappointed. They do not have what I need. Nor do I think they have what you need.

I want to learn by studying, then by testing and practicing and doing what the billion dollar traders do. I then want to figure out ways to explain it clearly and with passion, and back it up with a functional learning process to help the average person excel and spend more time with their family; that's why I sell books, courses and workshops. That's why I get nothing out of what you do. That's why I have no investments for sale. You have "one" unbiased educator in your life who wants to help you climb the steps of financial success. I've experienced enough gut wrenching for all of us in the process of learning this valuable role.

"If money is your hope for independence, you will never have it. The only real security that a man will have in this world is a reserve of knowledge, experience, and ability."

~Henry Ford

I want to give you hope and help qualify you for the American Dream.

INDISPUTABLE RULE #10
RULES RULE

Sorry to get cliche with you, but in the modem vernacular this says it all. "Teach me the rules and I'll play your game" (Anonymous). Can you imagine trying to play a game without knowing the rules? It would be tough. In fact, I believe most rules cause you to play better. Serving the right way in ping-pong causes you to be a much better server. It is that way in games as it is in life.

I firmly believe there are rules to living. I have found none better than those found in the Bible. I wrote extensively on these in four of my books: *A +*, *Success: American Style*, *Don't Set Goals* and my New York Times Business Best Selling book, *Business Buy the Bible.* One of the cause and effect rules of having *Business Buy the Bible* so popular was the intense negative comments by people who want to discard the Bible. Oh well, that's for a different discussion.

The point is that God has rules. Life has rules. Financial success has rules. My passion for life is to discover them, search them out, learn them inside out, use them and then help others learn and follow them. Success follows the person who follows the rules.

Understanding this leads me to my last point of all these ten rules: We need two things to achieve success: (I) A set of principles (values) to live by; and (2) A horse to ride on.

It matters not whether we're into sheet metal or sheet rock, into real estate or stocks, into cleaning up in business or being a janitor and cleaning up a business, the important things are eternally important, not fleeting. Achieving great results is simple: when we learn the rules of any enterprise (and learn and apply them well) great results will follow. If we can learn the system (the cause and effect) of any business or investment, then we can also learn and follow the rules of lasting value.

My mission, my personal passion in life, is not to write another stock market book or teach another seminar (though I have many more to come, as that is the horse I've chosen to ride), but to speak up and speak out, to remind and help people to return to that which is truly important.

SUMMARY: Rules are Tools

These are my ten rules for success. These Ten Indisputable Rules are also tools:

(1) Walk with wise people
(2) Use Passion and Precision to get the Profits you desire
(3) Blend Cash Flow; Tax Write-offs and Growth
(4) Learn from experience, but use the experiences and wisdom of others
(5) Use maintenance skills, not just acquisition skills
(6) Protect yourself against the three enemies of wealth
(7) Make money in bite-size pieces
(8) Change, grow into new profits
(9) Learn the price to be paid—focus on results.
(10) Rules Rule.

I am sure that successful people use rules, methods and systems as tools. Their tool chests are not only full of tools, but they have learned how to use each tool skillfully. They realize that different tools are used for different functions. Tools allow us to get far greater results (leverage) than using bare hands. The use of tools is a learnable skill. The results achieved measure up to the skill used.

My seven stock market income formulas are tools. Each of these seven stock market formulas has a function: a time and place to be used. Some can be used in combination with others. The skills to use these seven tools wisely are learnable. These tools can add strength and depth to what we are doing. Few stock market retail professionals even know these tools exist, let alone the fine points of usage. These tools have been developed over years of trial and error and perfected on-the-job.

I hate losing money! My strategies for making money are designed to stop any cash flow drains or any reduction in asset value. A lot of what I do is defensive in nature.

Develop and increase your enthusiasm for formulas, rules and methods and thereby stay on a clear path of wise financial decisions. I call this progress towards perfection. I hope I can help.

Abundantly Yours,

Wade B. Cook

HERE IS A LETTER FROM WADE'S WIFE LAURA:
I hope you realize the importance of what you have just read, and what you have the opportunity of obtaining.

Wade has concisely encapsulated his 24 years in the real estate, stock market, seminar and publishing worlds. What a wealth of experience is available to you in this book and even more so in his home study courses.

I am often asked what it is like to be married to Wade. He is dynamic in every aspect of his life. He has learned many lessons, often through painful trial and error, and is willing and anxious to share with you and have you benefit from the knowledge and experience he has gained. Why? I'll add my own Indisputable Rule: It's lonely at the Top! It is so much more gratifying for Wade to see students prosper than it is for him to prosper in a vacuum. The joy he gets from seeing your success and hearing your testimonials is indescribable. Being able to share his abundance of knowledge is where he feels the most success.

Don't pass up this opportunity to tap into one of the most brilliant minds in the country. THIS IS WADE COOK!

BONUS SECTION
HOW DO YOU LEARN BEST?

Read this exciting marketing piece and see if our "experiential learning" event is right for you.

IS WADE COOK'S WALL STREET WORKSHOP REALLY AS GOOD AS PEOPLE SAY?

"Wade Cook has a near genius way of taking something very complex and making it simple to understand and follow."

~ Mark Haroldsen
Author of *The Courage to Be Rich*

"To succeed extravagantly you have to study and be a mentee to a master mentor . . . Wade Cook is one of the masters of our time, and you will get every good thing you want."

~ Mark Victor Hansen
Co-Author of *Chicken Soup for the Soul*

Every once in awhile an event comes around which is so cutting edge, so state-of-the-art, and so pertinent that we just had to be a part of it, and one to which we want to share with our students, our clients, our associates. Wade Cook's Wall Street Workshop is a comprehensive and brilliantly formatted "smorgasbord" of detailed financial strategies for creating wealth and enhancing cash flow.

The techniques within this two day will shatter stale, old-fashioned, boring methods. It is said, "Genius has a way of lighting its own fire." Maybe some of Wade's knowledge and enthusiasm needs to rub off on you.

We acknowledge Wade Cook is one of the most controversial men in America. It's almost comical to read the press from "status quo" mucky-mucks who know nothing of the real world, and have so much to lose when Wades ideas to take hold.

Albert Einstein said, "Geniuses have always had violent opposition from mediocre minds." We invite you to bring your attorneys, your CPA's, your stock market and real estate brokers—but only if they can deal with their worlds being rocked.

"*This seminar taught me how to start with a small amount of cash and build it up into the large nest egg that I want. All my dreams can come true with the Wade Cook strategies. He should be teaching at the Harvard Business School. They never taught me anything like this.*"

~ Jack C. CA

"*The door just opened. I hope that everyone in this seminar was as enlightened as I. I had no idea what potential "the market" held within it, although I have been trading for year . . . I am grateful that I will no longer be "gambling" in the market, but profiting off of those who are.*"

~ Dr. Lee C., TX

"*Since taking the course, we have been terrifically successful in employing Wade's strategies. So successful that I have stopped practicing law after 30 years.*"

~ Bill K., CO

"*I feel like I have been reading by candlelight. Now, someone turned on the overhead and I see the big picture.*"

~ Marie N., AL

This bonus section will ask several questions frequently asked about our unique "Experiential Learning" Wall Street Workshop—A Real Trading Bootcamp. We use student testimonials to help make our case.

There is an old proverb which says, "The biggest fish you'll ever catch is still swimming in the ocean." Really think about this sentence, because the most money you are ever going to make has not been made yet.

Your best stock market, real estate or business transaction is still in your future. As we go through this educational report, you will be presented with the knowledge and opportunity that will be of utmost importance regarding your financial future. We'll start by exploring the question. Can you still get rich in America Today? Read the question again, putting the emphasis on a different word each time. Which meaning is most important to you? Is it the fact that you can still get rich, or that you can get rich, or that you can get rich today? If you choose the word still, meaning that people have gotten rich in the past and wonder if they can still get rich, using old-fashioned methods, or are there new ways to get wealthy today?

The real emphasis, however, as far as we are concerned, is "you." We devote everything to telling, showing, and setting the example for "you." Let's explore our educational format in this bonus section, and see if a good marriage can be made between us. You want to find out what it takes to get rich, and we have as our mission in life to educate people on strategies to help them get rich in American now.

CAN BIG BUCKS (LIKE MILLIONS) BE MADE IF I'M WILLING TO PAY THE PRICE?

We'll let our students answer this question. You determine how much and when to slow down:

"*I had $36,000 and turned it into $460,000 in less than 3 months. In another account, I took $100,000 and turned it into $400,000 in 4 weeks, and in another, I made $30,000 in one week for a total (account balance) of $960,000.*"

~ John T., OK

"*I turned $200,000 approximately into $1,200,000 in 6 months.*"

~ Larry G., CA

"*I made $1,338,081.43 net profit in 11 ½ months. I originally started with $36,000.*"

~ Mike L., WA

"I recently took an account from $16,000 to $330,000 in 2 weeks, and $35,000 to $2,484,000 in 6 weeks. I made 1.2 million in one day."

~ Glenn M., IL

"My wife and I started trading with about $30,000 and have now three accounts in the hundreds of thousands. I will be leaving my job of 34 years later this year and will continue to trade for a living. You, Wade, have changed my life. My wife and I are graduates and (are) making more money that we could ever have dreamed of."

~ Paul P., IL

WHAT DO FINANICAL PROFESSIONALS SAY ABOUT WADE COOK'S WALL STREET WORKSHOP.

"I am a licensed broker (Series 6, 63, and Series 7) and, by position, I am a broker assistant for (a major bank). I have been employed there since June of '99. I took that job to learn about investing/money management, which I have since learned that they don't know. Thanks for teaching me in 3 days what they couldn't teach me in 8 months."

~ Derek S., MI

"I have a background as a stockbroker and have been investing for about 15 years. I thought I knew how to make money in the market, but I wasn't even CLOSE!"

~ Neil P., WA

"I am a licensed general securities broker, licensed insurance agent, and CFP (Certified Financial Planner). And compared to (the instructor) I don't know jack! It just proves that institutional knowledge and street knowledge is about a $100,000 plus per year difference in money making capability. Bravo Wade Cook Strategies."

~ Christopher K., FL

"As a former stockbroker and current commodity broker, everything I ever wanted to do to help people make money in the markets was here at the Wall Street Workshop. This is a dream come true for me and I can never truly explain how much of an impact was made on me today."

~ Richard M., FL

You've all heard of "income producing assets." For most of you, you are your only incoming producing asset. And if your asset doesn't show up for work, there is no income. Our Workshop is about creating and developing another grouping of assets, which will produce the income you need to live on.

There are many (critics, stockbrokers, journalists) who say, "Hey Americans, you're stupid. You can't understand the machinations of the market. Give us your money. We'll manage it (for many fees). We'll take care of your money for you."

Then along comes Wade Cook, a cab driver, who says, "Hold it Americans! You are smart enough. You can learn and do these things. You can take your financial life into your own hands. I'll learn the formulas, distill them down, and help you learn. You can do it without fancy computers. You can do it without a lot of money to get started. And you can do it in a way that keeps your money safe while you learn, and then, earn with your real money. Many financial professionals don't want you to know the truth. Perhaps your own stockbrokers don't even know these things."

The road to wealth is not difficult if you have the right priorities. We want to help. We'll stick with you until you make it!

We're not big into goal setting; we're big into goal getting. Now, even in Wade's book *Don't Set Goals (The Old Way)*, he talks about being the type of person who achieves success.

One of the things all successful people have in common is they know where they want to end up. . .at the end of the day, at the end of the year, and the end of their life. Now, those priorities might change from time to time, but at any given time, they know what they want.

As a matter of fact, this was number one of H.L. Hunt's For Ways to Achieve Financial Success. He was interviewed by a journalist shortly before he died. Now remember, he is the man who was one of the richest men in the world. He was worth over three-billion dollars. The journalist asked him, "How do you get rich?" His answer, "There are four steps: 1) Know what you want: 2) know what you are willing to give up: 3) set your priorities: and 4) **Be** about it."

Let's say you know what you want. You're in the military, and you need to get your troops (money) safely across a minefield. You know how dangerous it can be, but you must get to the other side. Let's look at possible scenarios.

Scenario #1: Someone is on the edge of the minefield. He will tell you where to step. From a distance, he may even point out where a few of the mines are hidden. He wants $500 for this information.

Scenario #2**:** Someone is on the edge of the minefield and has a map for sale. The map shows a path through the minefield—where you can go and not get blown up. He wants $1,000 for the map.

Scenario #3: Another man explains that he has been across the minefield and knows the way. He is willing to take you by the hand and let you follow in his footsteps. Literally guide you through, step by step, the path you need to use and avoid danger and stay in the safe areas. He wants $5,000 for taking you across.

Which one would you choose? Obviously, the person who has been in the minefield and knows the danger areas and can keep you in the safe areas is of extreme value.

We hope you'll give us a look as the company that will help you get to where you want to go. We don't sit back and draw maps. We are in the minefield everyday. We are not some elite, central command center, but a group of foxhole sergeants who are in the battle daily and are willing to take you by the hand and help you get to the other side. We are one unbiased company which can help you achieve what you want.

Before we continue, we would like to introduce you to Wade Cook and his TV remote control. Let's read from one of his previous stories:

"We have Direct TV at our home. It is hooked up to our TV which is hooked up with a VHS, DVD, and stereo system. My wife and son point, click, relax and enjoy the show. Not me, I can sit there for 30 minutes moving buttons, pushing, clicking, and then step 5—go get my wife or my son to help me get my show on."

I ask them for help! They grab the remote gadget and in 6 to 10 seconds the show is on. I say, "No, let me hold it!" At first, they reached over my shoulder and pushed the buttons. I was frustrated. I said, "No—stand over there and tell me how to do it. Let me push the buttons. Let me learn how to do it myself."

It was hard for them, I know, to let me do it myself. I need to see it done. I didn't need to read directions, I had done that. I didn't need a lecture, I had received several. I learn best by experience. It reminds me of our "TELL, SHOW, DO" process of education. That's how we teach. You, as a student, study, practice, understand and do.

We all learn best by doing. We learn best by experience. As an educational company, Liberty Network, Inc. wants to be head and shoulders above everyone else in the education field. Because our program does not provide students with options to get government assistance, or qualify for traditional college scholarships and other things like that, our students need to really want to be with us. As a matter of fact, we kind of pride ourselves in the fact that we have nothing for sale. You are reading this bonus section right now, but to take advantage of anything we have to offer, you're going to have to pick up the phone and call us. We provide you the information, but you have to buy from us. We hope you see the value in buying knowledge. Knowledge, especially cash flow knowledge, is truly the gift that keeps on giving.

Wade has put together a three-step educational process. It would not be very easy in a short report like this, to tell you that we have the coolest financial cash flow formulas available in the stock market. Don't get me wrong, we do have the coolest financial formulas—but that is not the secret to our success in helping you be successful. You might think that because we have a great internet site, where people can look over our shoulders and watch our trades being done, that this is the secret to our student's success. It's very important, but it is not the underlying key to our process.

What it is then that makes us unique is simply the style, the method, and the way that we help people get through the learning process. Now, think this one through from your perspective. Do you learn best by reading? Because some people do. You may learn best by hearing—a lot of people love listening to audio CDs, because hearing words is what is needed to imbed these formulas firmly in their minds. Do you learn best by seeing? For example, seeing live-action or action taken on video. OR, do you learn best by doing it yourself, experiencing the action? Many people learn best by doing. It's kind of the difference between reading a cookbook and actually using the recipe to make the meal.

Again, the question is, "How do you learn best?" We have found that many people need a holistic approach to this financial educational process. If we can bring together the written word, the spoken word and the experience, it promotes an extremely efficient level of understanding and results. In fact, we call this K.U.R.E. process. Our company truly does have the K.U.R.E.

You get the Knowledge, Understanding, Results and the Evaluation, which then keeps repeating and producing better results. As you evaluate, you move right back through the cycle again—it becomes knowledge for the next level, and the cycle never stops.

Can you see how we have "found success in helping you be successful?" You need the KURE, we have the KURE! Come and be a part of this wonderful learning experience.

In a previous written piece, Wade talked about an experience he had in getting ready to go into the studio to do a recording to send out to our students. Let's go there:

"I was scheduled to go into the recording studio. I was supposed to talk about the Wall Street Workshop and how it was a unique and completely successful seminar across the nation. I thought long and hard about what to say. I had to putt of the recording for several weeks. Finally, one morning at about 4 AM it came to me. It was simple. I should get off my side of the fence, as an educator, and tell you what I would want, as a student in a Wall Street Workshop."

I laid there and came up with three things that I would want, even demand from a seminar. Think these through with me and think about what type of seminar you would design for yourself if you had the chance.

FIRST: I would want to know what's available. What type of trades can be made in different situations? Even though I might not know much about the market, I do realize there are beginning, intermediate, and advanced methods. What can I use? Can I take the powerful formulas the "big guys" use and simplify them for my own benefit?

But to keep it simple, I thought, let's go back to the basics. You're just starting to learn baseball. There's one out, a runner on first and you've never played the infield. The coach yells, "Okay, double play—c'mon guys, double it up."

Can you do a double play if you don't know what a forced out is? That is what I mean by "know what is available." What if there are double plays in the stock market, much like baseball, with fixed plays and specific formulas on specific movements?

SECOND: I want to see the deals done. If I were a beginner to these strategies, I would want to see them done over and over again. I would want examples. I would want to see it work under different circumstances. I would want to see what happens when the trade doesn't go the way we planned. I would want to study and practice the trades. I would want to ask questions and move from knowledge or information to a true understanding.

THIRD: I want to do the deals myself. If paper trading or simulation trading will protect my money as I go through the learning curve, then fine. But, I want the experience to look and feel real. I realize that experience is the best teacher, but it is a truly wise person who can learn through the eyes (mistakes) of another.

In short, **I want to get results**. I want to move on to application and learn how to keep practicing so when it's time to use real money, I'm ready with a wealth of knowledge and a chest full of understanding to build confidence and overcome fear.

I was excited to get into the studio that day. I was on our students' side of the fence. I practiced what I was to say all the way to the office. Then it dawned on me that I had just discovered the other side of the educational coin I was so dedicated to working. Look at the following

HOW I WANT TO TEACH

1) TELL: Teach the strategies
2) SHOW: Use examples, discuss, explore
3) DO: Watch over student's activities

WHAT I WANT AS A STUDENT

1) Learn what's available—what works and when
2) Be shown examples and get explanations from someone who walks the walk
3) Do the deals with someone to help me understand how to get consistent results.

CAN I GET STARTED WITH VERY LITTLE MONEY?

"I attended a (Wall Street Workshop) in July of 1998. I didn't have any more money to start an account with, so I paper traded for six months.

As a single mom, finishing a degree, I finally found an on-line firm who would accept me with no required minimum balance. I started in February '99 with $200...My first trade on a stock (VRTL) netted me $9.00. Not a lot, but with more time than money, I studied hard and really concentrated on technicals. I turned that $200 into $6,200. (I added $500 tax return in May.) As of August 1st to September 8th, I've increased that to $9,000 doing Rolling Stock and some Covered Calls since July 1st."

~ Jodi L.

WHAT DO WE DO FOR TWO DAYS?

Another thing we have learned is that everyone learns differently. One person may learn best by listening. Plug this person into our CD training courses and they take off to the moon! Soon they're out buying stocks and options, making lots of money and having a lot of fun doing it.

Another person may like pictures, visual aids, and graphic representations. Put them in front of the TV with one of our video training courses, and they are in heaven. If they don't understand something, they rewind and replay until they do.

Others may have a fondness for the written word, letting each concept settle gradually into their minds. Still others learn better from experience. I contend to you that they best way to learn is a combination of all four methods.

Reading, enhanced by listening, enhanced further by seeing, and finally solidified by experience! This experiential learning is what makes our Wall Street Workshop students so successful. We tell you what to do, we then show you how to do it, and finally, we look over your shoulder as you do it.

HERE'S A BREAKDOWN OF OUR THREE FOLD "TELL-SHOW-DO" FORMAT

TELL: The educational facilitator explains the particular strategy—the beginning, middle and end—in detail. They go through the vocabulary and definitions, so you have a good working knowledge of the stock market jargon. They explain the different rules we have discovered that make this particular strategy work.

SHOW: The instructor, having now armed you with the basic information, moves to the next level of actually showing you how the transaction works. This involves several things, including placing the trade—either real or paper—so that you see how it is done, how it works. If time allows in the Workshop, multiple examples are executed, because repetition creates confidence in application.

DO: Now the facilitator will watch over the students as they are excused to go and do deals on their cell phones or to the phones in the hallways to place real or simulated trades. Again, our Workshop is to help people practice perfectly, so that when it is time to use real money, they are up-to-speed, in-the-know and on-the-go. One of the things we do is help our students keep their money out of harm's way. That's why our class—even though many people do real trades—is designed to teach people how to Simutrade, to get good on paper, before they use their own hard-earned cash.

The Tell, Show, Do format is a wonderful process that helps students get through the learning curve quickly. Our job is not to make good Workshop attendees out of our students, but to make them good when they get home and are with their own trading professionals. You simply need to learn how to do this. The Wall Street Workshop is a two day event. It is not a seminar, but a roll-up-your-sleeves, "do-the-deals" workshop. Our instructors will use newspapers, charting services, brokers or our trading department on the phone, to not only tell you how to make money, but to show you how to do it, and then watch over you while you do it yourself. We make money in class, either real or simulated using actual numbers. It is education at its powerful best. Read what our students learn and do:

"I turned $200,000 approximately into 1.2 million in 6 months."

~ Larry G., CA

"I trade full time, (bought) a 6 bedroom home with swimming pool and tennis court, helped others who needed work (they work on my house now and I pay them with what I make in the market). I know if I lost everything, I could start with enough to buy one contract and make it from there."

~ Garland H., FL

A COMMON COMMENT WE RECEIVE IS THAT MORE MONEY IS MADE THAN WHAT THEY PAID FOR TUITION.

"I have spent a lot of money for my education of the stock market through the Wade Cooks seminars and feel that in every class I got much more than my money's worth. I have learned so much and have been able to take what I learned and make enough money to pay for the classes...I feel I learned and experienced much more than what I paid for."

~ Rosalie W., WA

"This is the second time that I have taken the course. I took the first (one) three weeks ago and I have made $10,000! This works! I am living proof!"

~ Kimberly H., OR

"I found Wade in desperation. I invested approximately $100,000 in stock between a few lousy (I know this now!) brokers. Within a whopping 6 months, I have a grand total of $50,000. Thanks to taking it upon myself to manage my money with Wade's strategies, I've earned $25,000 back in two months (while being very conservative).

~ Michael B., CA

Get in the flow. You cannot get rich on a mental desert island.

Surround yourself with achievers. Lose the losers. May we humbly ask that you consider, as an alternative to the old rut you're in, a new place to go and a new group to hang out with—yes, Wade. We're not perfect but we're students first, educators second. We are doing what we teach and teaching what we do. We are always improving and all this to your benefit.

WE WANT YOU EXCITED AGAIN!! Not so excited by what we teach as by what you'll be able to DO. Again, it's not what we teach, but how we teach—indeed, it is how you learn that makes all the difference in the world.

Here's the best part—the tuition for the Wall Street Workshop is just $5,295. With 300 to 400 potentially new and exciting methods, tips, techniques, and tools available, that's about $20 per technique. Each method could make you $10,000 or more. You'll see that it could easily cost you $100,000 or more not to attend—it's just that good.

Also, at the time this report; we have a few tuition discounts, add-ons and bonuses. Call for details.

You have read what the Wall Street Workshop is all about. You have read testimonials from students. Not just testimonials about how much money people are making, but how much this workshop has changed their lives. When you really think about what "financial freedom" is, isn't it the ability to be in control of your life, doing what you want to do when you want? Let's face it, our bills will never go away and out needs are always increasing. Each of us can use more cash flow. The American Dream is alive and well. We want to help you turn dreams gone blue into dreams come true.

We have what you need. We purvey quality information for your results and for your benefit. Don't delay your success.

WE STAND BY READY TO HELP,
THE NEXT MOVE IS YOURS

Call for space availability, tuition discounts (if available) scholarship credits, and course bonuses. We have surrounded you with knowledge that truly makes a difference. Call 1-866-579-5900 to speak with an enrollment Director and register for the Wall Street Workshop.

 For information on topics contained within this brochure call 866-579-5900

Liberty Network, Inc.
#2131
1420 NW Gilman Blvd
Issaquah, WA 98027

"***Your family is too important, your retirement too close, to leave your future up to chance. Take this Bull Market by the horns and make good things happen***."

~ Wade B. Cook

"Victory is not won in miles but in inches. Win a little now, hold your ground, and later win a little more."

~ Louis L'Amour

APPENDIX
RESOURCE MATERIALS

STOCK MARKET BOOKS:
Some of these books are available from the publisher only.

Wall Street Money Machine (Revised Edition):

The book that changed the way America bought and sold stock! Hailed by beginners and experts alike! All the great information you loved in the classic edition. This revised and updated version is a great introduction for creating wealth using the Wade Cook formulas.

- Aggressive strategies for making cash flow in the stock market—Rolling Stocks, Covered Calls, Stock Splits and more.
- Inside secrets—find out the inside secrets to stock options and turn them into a cash flow machine.
- Proxy Investing—Make money on stock you can't afford (yet).
- Combined strategies—Rolling Options, double dipping, "overdrive" and more.
- Protect your assets—Learn the strategies so you can keep more of what you make.

Plus all new:

- Charts and examples
- Even more money making ideas!
- Covered Calls, even more in-depth
- Options explored and explained like never before!

Stock Market Miracles:
Finally, a book by an author that understands what the average investor needs: knowing when to sell. The information in this book will give you the ability to make money using real tried-and-true techniques. No special knowledge required, no strings attached. These tools can help you secure real wealth. Thanks to Wade Cook, financial miracles happen every day for thousands of students who are applying what they have learned from this book. Buy it today and see what miracles happen in your life.

Bulls and Bears:
You learn and apply these cash-flow strategies regardless of whether the market is trending up, down or sideways. Wade Cook took Wall Street by storm. His best selling book, Wall Street Money Machine, Vol 1, gave hope to old and new investors alike with innovative formulas to make big time bucks. Now comes *Bulls and Bears*, to shatter the myopic vision of the bearish commentators who are constantly predicting a downturn in the market. This book will elevate your thinking and give you the tools to make money regardless of the market. Don't miss this insightful look into what makes bull and bear markets and how to make exponential returns in any market.

In this book you'll learn how to:

- Avoid (or use) negativism—turn bearish symptoms to your advantage
- See the potential for cash flow in any market—recognize market trends and know how to use them.
- Play both peaks and valleys—make money on the ups and downs
- Use formulas to generate income—get in and out of deals quickly for maximum profits
- Build a solid portfolio of top producing stocks—choose the right stocks for superior long term growth.

Free Stocks: How to Get the Stock Market to Pay for your Stocks:
Wade Cooks wants the stock market paying for your stocks! If you like the buy and hold strategy of investing, how do you get the money to pay for your stock? Wade Cook demonstrates how to get the market to pay for your stock within five to seven months using his NEW LOCC system. Learn how to start building the portfolio of your dreams for FREE!

In Free Stocks, you will find out about:

- Options Cycles and Market Makers
- How Implied Volatility Affects Option Pricing
- Buybacks and Rollouts
- Stock Repair Kit—Fix broken stocks with added income
- How to put volatility on your side—Be a seller, not a buyer
- When you get your money
- Exploration of ways to increase gains and reduce taxes
- What to do if the stock dips—make more money!

Red Light, Green Light
Once more best selling author Wade Cook delivers financial education no one else is providing. Take back control of your cash-flow from retail stockbrokers, who simply do not know about the quarterly "newsy-go-round"—Red Light Green Light, shows you how, why, and when to trade for the best profits using this reporting cycle. Use this book to bring your stock market actions alive! Benefit from the following topics:

- No News is Bad News
- Making Better Trades
- Strategies and Attitudes for Success
- Increasing your powers of observation
- Strategies for Red Light, Green Light periods
- Using Red Light, Green Light for cash flow
- Compelling reasons means cash profits
- Red Light, Green Light and Stock Splits

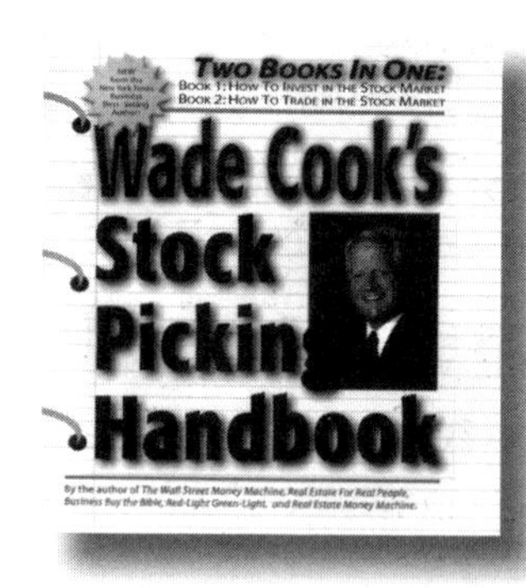

Wade Cook's Stock Picking Handbook: Two Books in One

The time is now. Good values exist. The formulas, methods and strategies for investing and trading in the market are in this book.

Book One: How to Invest in the Stock Market

- What makes stocks go up
- How to choose stocks wisely
- The law of supply and demand
- Follow earnings: the infamous P/E ratios
- Buy and hold is a strategy whose time has come and gone
- Events which move stocks and the January effect
- Stock Repair Kit—How to fix stocks
- Sailing the seven "C"s
- A P/E ratio update on finding values
- The quarterly news/ no news cycles

Book Two: How to Trade in the Stock Market

- Writing Covered Calls—the 20% monthly cash flow challenge
- Options 101: a primer
- Selling in-the-money covered calls for more consistent cash flow
- Trade suitability—make the right trade
- RECIPES—Let's cook up some deals (ingredients, mixing instructions, baking time)
  a) Blue Chocolate Chip Cookies
  b) Rolling Stocks: Refrigerator Cookies
  c) Options: Cream Puffs
  d) Stock Split Muffins
  e) Covered Calls: Icing on the Cake
  f) Seafood Smorgasbord—Bottom Fishing

REAL ESTATE AND OTHER BOOKS

How to Pick Up Foreclosures: HOT OFF THE PRESS!!

The time is right. Bargains are everywhere. The formulas, methods and strategies for investing and trading in today's real estate market are in this book.

- Using the time line to your benefit
- Get there first—Capture the deal
- An Investors Dream: Leverage at Bargain Prices
- Step-by-step processes that really work in today's market
- How to evaluate properties
- Pitfalls to Avoid

In How to Pick Up Foreclosures, Wade Cook, America's premier rags to riches educator takes you through every step of purchasing foreclosures. He tells you what has worked for him and explains how you can create your own real estate cash flow system.

Real Estate for Real People:

Learn strategies for a lifetime of income. A priceless, comprehensive overview of real estate investing, this book teaches you how to buy the right property for the right price, at the right time. Wade Cook explains all of the strategies you'll need and gives you twenty reasons why you should start investing in real estate today. Learn how to retire rich with real estate, and have fun doing it.

101 Ways to Buy Real Estate Without Cash

The real secret in getting your money out of a property is to not put any money into the property in the first place! In 101 Ways to Buy Real Estate Without Cash, author Wade Cook shows you innovative strategies that let you pay little to nothing down to make a lot of money.

Filled with 101 creative ways to buy real estate without cash, this is an invaluable book for new and experienced investors alike. Perhaps the most valuable idea book you'll ever read.

Learn innovative ways to:

- Put the seller in the driver's seat while maintaining control of the offer
- Invest with others and combine your strengths for even greater returns
- Lower the down payment and price of the house
- Create and trade paper for equity or cash

These tips and a dozen more innovative ideas will give you an overflowing toolbox from which to choose just the right tool for making your fortune, and teach you how to get in with a dime and out with a dollar!

Wealth 101

Wade Cook taught you how to invest in both real estate and the stock market. Now in Wealth 101, he teaches strategies and techniques to help you create, manage and maintain wealth in all areas of investments. This book is a comprehensive guide to get you started on the road to riches. You can't afford not to read this book.

Tax Strategies for Network Marketers (Excerpts from formerly titled Brilliant Deductions)

Do you want to make the most of the money you earn? If you want to have solid tax havens and ways to reduce the taxes you pay, this book is for you. It will teach you how to get rich in spite of the new tax laws and by doing network marketing. Read about new tax credits, year-end maneuvers, and methods for transferring and controlling your entities. Learn to structure yourself and your family for tax savings and liability protection.

Real Estate Money Machine

"Every once in a while a book comes along with a new idea, a novel approach and logical answers to the problems of times. Wade Cook's book, Real Estate Money Machine, is such a book."

~ Robert Allen,
author of Nothing Down.

Concise strategies that really work. That's what investors—experienced and inexperienced alike—want. Real knowledge, obtained from real experience, that really works. And, that's what Wade Cook gives you in this practical how-to-book. He shows you, the reader, how to do what he's done, only better. He pours everything he knows, the good and the bad, into the Real Estate Money Machine. He'll teach you how to develop your own real estate money machine by following his easy-to-apply strategies.

PERSONAL DEVELOPMENT BOOKS

A+

A+ is a collection of wisdom, thoughts, and principles of success which can help you make millions, even billions of dollars and live an A+ life. As you will see, Wade Cook constantly tries to live his life in the second mile, to do more than asked, to be above normal. If you want to live a successful life, you need great role models to follow. For years, Wade Cook's life has been a quest to find successful characteristics of his role models and implement them in his own life. In A+, Wade will encourage you to find and incorporate the most successful principles and characteristics of success in your life, too. You will learn:

- How to emulate successful characteristics
- The importance of great role models
- How to get and stay enthused
- How to have financial success
- Hints on the road to being rich
- Help in answering, "Is it a sin to be wealthy? or poor?
- How your hands are an extension of your heart
- Where and how to find true happiness

Learn how Wade Cook has experienced an A+ life and how you can too! Don't spend another day living less than an A+ life.

Business Buy the Bible

Inspired by the Creator, The Bible truly is the authority for running the business of life. Throughout this book I provide you, the reader, with practical advice that helps you apply God's word to your life. Wades goal is to teach people everywhere how to become wealthy so that they can lead their lives in service to God, their families, and others.

Power Quotes

Wade Cook knows the impact of words. Throughout his life, Wade has found comfort and inspiration in the words of those who have experienced life and prospered. To this day, he continues to memorize specific quotes he finds the most inspiring. Because he had dedicated his life to teaching ordinary people how to experience the same extraordinary success he has, Wade has compiled this book as a way to give everyone access to the inspiration from the best minds ever. As many of you already know, Wade believes that you cannot learn to succeed by listening to anyone who is not already a success. The authors quoted in this book are the successful people Wade is listening to. If you want to succeed you cannot afford to miss the incredible opportunity to have the advice of some of the most successful minds ever in your hands. Make it a point to start every day with a burst of wisdom to help guide you through life's obstacles.

Don't Set Goals

Be-ing! Prioritize and get into action. It is important to be moving in the right direction. This book tells you how taking action and "paying the price" is more important than simply making the decision to do something. Don't set goals. Go out and simply get where you want to go!

Call now for prices and specials 866-579-5900 or check our www.libertynetwork.us All these book are available by the publisher only!!!

S.M.A.R.T.
SMART (STOCK MARKET ACCELERATED RETURNS TRAINING)

This is one of the best educational package deals you are ever going to find. This market has been a strange one, as of late, no doubt. We were losing money just like everyone else, but we found out what we were doing wrong and we FIXED IT. This package covers some of the strategies we used to climb out of the market quagmire and rise above the confusion to turn our account around. In this 18 CD Set you will find more detailed information about Investing vs. Trading, Option Basics, Write Up Your Income, BO-ST (Buy One Sell Two), LOCC (Large Option Covered Calls), Up Your Profits, Building Family Wealth. So don't wait to get this package today and turn your life into a life of purpose.

Investing vs. Trading **$259 but for readers of this book $159**
This is a time of opportunity. The market says "trade." The low P/E's spell value. Yes, the market has changed, BUT don't miss this chance to learn, relearn, and oftentimes unlearn lessons of the past and get to the "now." Wade Cook is in the trenches every day, trying, testing, adapting, improvising and improving.

We're UP. Ask yourself—do I want to learn how Wade Cook and his staff did this? Well, the answers are in this half-day unique course.

Put Wade's Knowledge and Real Life Experience to Work for You.

TOPICS:

- ✔ Trading vs. Investing
- ✔ Selling Volatility
- ✔ Position Trading Made Easy
- ✔ Focus on Commentary
- ✔ Focus on Exit Points
- ✔ Build A Quality Life.
- ✔ Selling Time
- ✔ Bargain Hunting
- ✔ Earnings Announcements
- ✔ Trading With A Purpose
- ✔ Build Consistent Cash Flow
- ✔ Getting Money In the Way Of Movements

LOCC Up Your Profits with Large Option Covered Calls
$279 but for readers of this book $179

You are 6 months 12 months or 18 months (depending on whether you start with $5,000, $15,000 or $25,000). This half day event is divided into two parts.

"LOCC Up Your Profits is a "lifestyle choice." It's the basis for Building Assets—and cash flowing those assets later"

—Wade B. Cook

- ✔ Pertinent
- ✔ Timely
- ✔ Powerful
- ✔ Functional

TOPICS:
- ✔ Covered Call Basics—And variations on a theme
- ✔ Choosing Better Stocks—Earnings Fundamentals (Note: This session alone is worth millions)
- ✔ Sell Large Premiums—Time and Volatility
- ✔ Passive—Let it run, 60% to 80% 6 month return
- ✔ Busy—Jump back in, buy back and roll out
- ✔ Enhance strategies for cash flow—switch to income

This one-of-a-kind event shows time-honored ways to build wealth. LOCC and LOAD—let's go!

Hundreds of Hints, Techniques and Strategies

Options 101 $249 but now $149.
Note: See combination price later!
Four Incredible Seminars in one. This is a must-have course for everyone. A comprehensive, step-by-step, learning extravangza. Four to five remarkable hours by Wade Cook and his 29,000 PLUS trades—truly making experience the best teacher.

CD #1: Option Basics—An Effective Start
CD #2: Option Pricing—Great Information
CD #3: Use Options Properly
CD #4: Selling Options—For consistent cash flow

TOPICS:

- ✔ Proxy Investing change the multiples—Getting wealthy the cash flow way
- ✔ Leverage, movements, pricing and profits
- ✔ Magnified movements—Making time you Friend
- ✔ Deteriorating premiums—Put this technique to work for your benefit
- ✔ Profit Opportunities: Buy or Sell—Putting market forces to work for you.
- ✔ Pitfalls to Avoid—Better entrance and exit points
- ✔ Safe Territory—Recon (enter the trade) Back to Safe Territory
- ✔ Surgical strikes—profit motive, In and Out with Focus. Rule of Three Strategy—3 good trades out of ten, and still make 20%—unique, powerful

WBC on WCC (Wade B. Cook on Writing Covered Calls)
$259 but for readers of this book $159
Everything You've Ever Wanted to Know About Writing Covered Calls. There are three reasons for investing: Cash Flow, Tax Write-offs and Growth

Let's focus on the CASH FLOW FIRST

Invest? Trade?

DON'T CHOOSE—Do Both—Trade on your investments. Skills in one enhance, the other.

EXTRA MONEY—Most Americans do now know how to generate extra monthly profits. Sad but true.

COVERED CALLS—Monthly cash flow machine—many angles and in-and-out profits.

TRADE ON INVESTMENTS—Use existing stock for actual cash generation. Do monthly or more.

CASH RETURNS—10% to 15% cash returns are not uncommon. Real life examples.

TOPICS:

- ✔ Option Pricing for selling—A covered call explained in detail
- ✔ Protecting the underlying investment—Manage the downside risk
- ✔ Buy in dips, sell for more profit—Extra work, but extra profits: wash, rinse, repeat
- ✔ Rolling Covered Calls—A student viewpoint for double dipping examples
- ✔ The incredible "Buy Back" worked in numerous examples.

BO-ST (Buy One Sell Two) $259 but for readers of this book $159

Here is a simple question: If you like the monthly income from covered call writing (selling), would you like to make an extra $400 to $800 per trade? No fooling. At 3 to 5 covered calls a month, that's an extra $2000 to $3000. Introducing Wade Cook's nearly infamous Buy One—Sell Two add on strategy. This half day event is loaded with examples, formulas, cautions and concerns and the in-depth know how to get this strategy pounding out more profits.

TOPICS:

- ✔Proxy Trade—The Bull Call Spread. Substitute Options
- ✔Match Up—Stock With Lower Strike Prices
- ✔Sell Twice as many upper-priced options
- ✔Create Covered Calls, Bull Call Spreads—Sometimes for no money
- ✔Double Profits—Often Give Yourself a Better Chance
- ✔Pitfalls to Avoid—Techniques, Hints and Concerns
- ✔Which Stocks Work the Best—Sell Volatility

BFW=Building Family Wealth $259 but for readers of this book $159

"Our purpose in life should be to build a life of purpose."

—Wade B. Cook

BFW . . . Gives you the detail methods for building a strong family dynasty

BFW . . . Explores wealth enhancement techniques which are state of the art

BFW . . . Is about "Current Real World" solutions to age old problems

BFW . . . Is simply a far reaching event with incredible consequences—both good if you follow the techniques and bad if you don't

Receive all 6 Volumes of SMART for $995 plus $15 S & H

HANDS ON TRAINING

All through this book you have been reading about TNT, TST and TDT. Here is a detailed explanation of all three. We present this here hoping you will subscribe.

TNT (Tuesday Night Training):
Liberty Network, Inc. lets you, from the comfort of your own home, with Wade Cook and other top educators, investors and traders, join in a lively evening presentation. Wade will teach an "in-the-trenches" tele-seminar on getting assets to produce income so you don't have to work so much. The topic is primarily "writing covered calls." However, many other aspects of working the market will be explored! The time is 6 PM Pacific, 9PM Eastern. This is a detailed "do-the-deals" event. If you're in doubt about the quality (can you do it) we'll give you one or two complimentary events so you can decide for yourself.

These events are simply wonderful:

- ✔ Techniques—Real Working knowledge
- ✔ Actual Trades—5 to 10 each week
- ✔ Street Wise tips, formulas and methods

These remarkable evening presentations are designed to help you increase your wealth and enhance your cash flow.

TST (Trading Skills and Techniques)
Look over the shoulder of Wade Cook and our staff as they do their trades. We also help you paper trade to really learn each technique and develop confidence. 24/7 you can log on to our website and be tutored through the deals. Watch Wade and his staff make money. No one puts their trades, commentary and thoughts out for the whole world to see. This alone lists for $200 per month, but is yours FREE with you TNT subscription.

- ✔ Explore, learn and earn
- ✔ See money made as it happens
- ✔ Log on 24/7—at your convenience
- ✔ Connect-the-dots—See Wade and the staff make the deals
- ✔ Win, Lose or Draw—our trades, with "why" and "how" commentary are given to help you when you need the help.

Here's how it works. As a Subscriber you will receive a PIN and PASSWORD. Just log on and see the deals done. Frequent (2 to 5 entries) are made every day. We're here to help you get your ASSETS PRODUCING CASH FLOW! Yes, every month.

TDT (Thousand Dollar Thursday)
$$ A GRAND NEW DEAL EVERY WEEK$$
Every Thursday we will send a one to two page email with tips and explanations of formulas, methods or deals—actual trades that will make $1,000. We take $4,000 to $5,000 and show you at least one $1,000 trade every week. Repeat $$A GRAND NEW DEAL EVERY WEEK$$. The list price for this invaluable information is $1295 per year, but again, yours FREE with your TNT subscription.

You saw sample TDT's and excerpts from TST earlier in the book. Check these out. Call now 866-579-5900.

Also note: Affiliate programs are available so you can make even more money.

NOTES:

All About: Stock Market Strategies
Market Timing

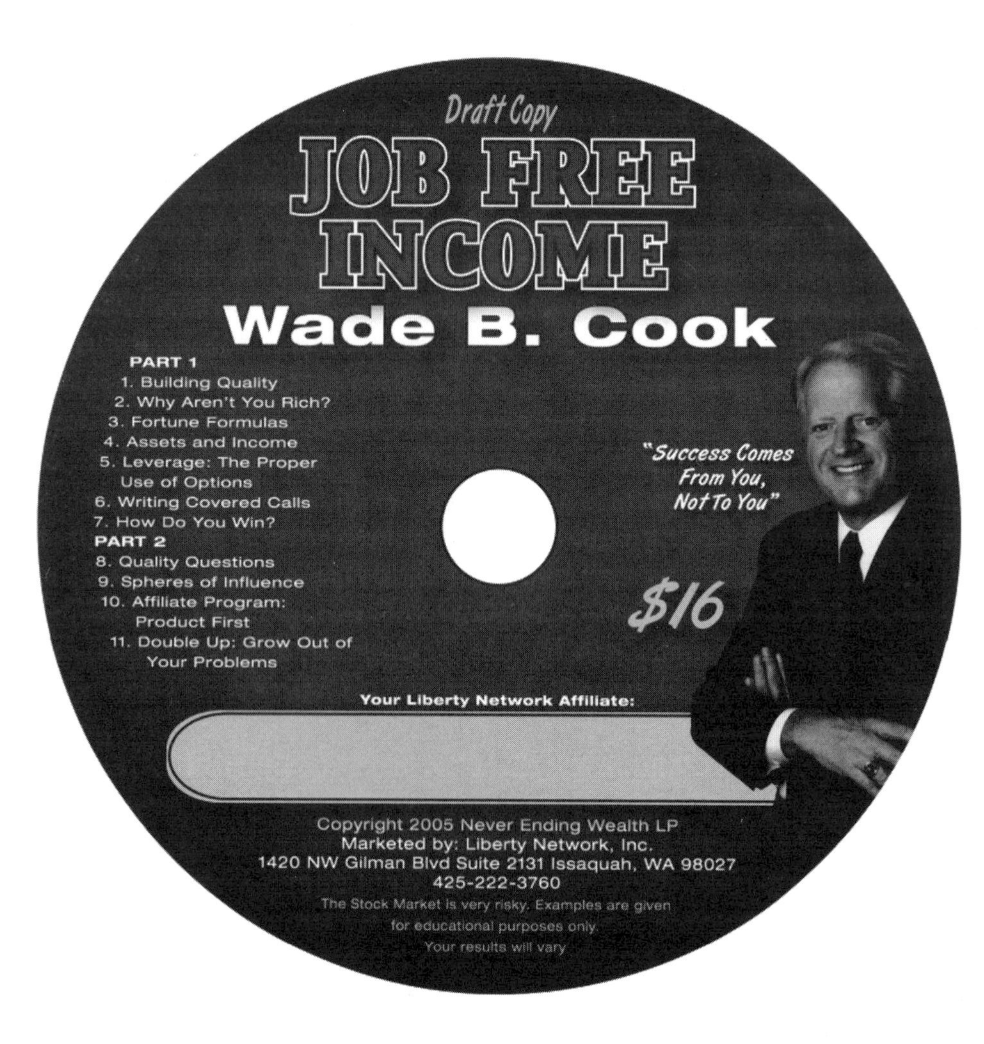

Note: If there is not a FREE CD—JOB FREE INCOME—in this book, please call 866-579-5900. This is a powerful, fast-paced seminar.

IT'S FREE—CALL NOW

Your Liberty Network, Inc. Affiliate